Life
with the
Coal Tar

*Stories from Campbeltown's
West Coast fisherfolk*

Freddy Gillies

Illustrations David Cowan

**Northern Books
from Famedram**

Printed and published in Scotland by Famedram Publishers,
Formartine AB41
© Copyright 1992, Famedram Publishers and Freddy Gillies.
Not to be reproduced in any form without permission.

ISBN: 0 905489 48 9

Contents

Thank you for joining me on this armchair fishing trip. The book is is no way intended to be a historical or technical account of the industry. Written entirely at sea during quiet spells, it is merely a sometimes lighthearted, sometimes serious look at my life as a fisherman sailing from ports on the Scottish West Coast.

I would like to thank the following people for their help and encouragement during the preparation of this book: Alison Chadwick and Finlay Oman of *The Scottish Fishing Weekly* for some of the photographs, Mrs Jane Pollock, Campbeltown and Miss Valerie Dudgeon, Oban

JAMIE RUSSELL

STEWART CAMPBELL

BILLY MARTINDALE

DOUGAL JOHN CAMPBELL

*In memory of the above-named close friends who lost their lives on the **MFV Antares,** tragically involved in an accident with HM Submarine **Trenchant** on November 23, 1990 in the Firth of Clyde.*

The author in sunny mood at Arbroath Harbour

Introduction

I FIRST went to sea on a fishing boat with skipper
Jim Meenan aboard the Campbeltown herring
ring-netter, **Stella Maris** (CN 158). The feeling of
sheer joy and exhilaration that was etched on my
nine-year-old mind has remained ever since.

Throughout my years in Campbeltown
Grammar School, navigation was unquestionably
my favourite subject. To myself and my classmates
it was something of a foregone conclusion that I
would become a fisherman at the earliest
opportunity. Or so we thought.

I hadn't reckoned on a set of parents taking a
somewhat different point of view. My elder brother
Robert was already at the fishing and Willie, three
years my junior, had made it plain that his future
lay at sea also. Since I was supposed to be 'good at
the school' my mother and father firmly insisted
that I find work ashore.

Amid adolescent protestations that the entire
world was against me I finally accepted defeat and,
in August 1966, embarked on a career as a news

reporter on the *Campbeltown Courier*. Suffice it to say I was to be found at the harbour as often as in the office.

It appeared I was destined for a life in journalism when, after three years on the *Courier*, I left my beloved Campbeltown for a post in the head office of a large evening newspaper in Wolverhampton, the *Express and Star*. I enjoyed two years covering 'big time' stories and got on well with my colleagues. Indeed, I shall always hold an affection for the paper, even though I was based in a place that could hardly be farther from the sea.

Life there was made bearable by the presence of another young Scottish journalist on the paper, Charlie Rae, from Plains, near Airdrie. We shared the same lodgings and spent off-duty hours in a relentless pursuit of female talent in the many clubs and discotheques which abound in Wolverhampton.

Indeed, we became known in the office as Laurel and Hardy, with me playing the part of Stan and Charlie, with a slightly rotund figure and dark Italian features inherited from his mother, an obvious Olly.

Charlie has gone on to become an important figure on the London media scene, travelling world-wide in search of headline making material for the *Today* newspaper.

It's not that I really disliked the area, but an incident involving a car I was immensely proud of finally set me on a northerly course home.

I was doing a story in Bradeley, a heavily industrialised Black Country town and had parked my car beside a foundry. I recall how odd it looked standing all on its own and on my return was mystified to see that a strange grey dust had settled on it. I thought no more about it until the following morning when I was struck dumb by the sight which greeted me. The paintwork had been stripped in parts to the bare metal, due, I found out later, to the fall-out from the foundry's stacks.

Clean air for me I decided, and handed in my resignation that same day. I don't think I looked back as the Euston-Glasgow train growled its way out of Wolverhampton High Level Station a few weeks later.

Much to my parents' chagrin, I had arranged with an uncle, skipper Ronnie Brownie, of nearby Carradale, to join his boat for the forthcoming herring season. I was acutely disppointed to learn on my homecoming that vital engine parts for the boat were missing in transit and I had to spend a frustrating three weeks until she was ready for sea.

During my first week home, I met an old friend, Frank Stacey, who was at that time between fishing berths. He suggested that to augment our finances and pass the time, we should indulge in a spot of whelk picking. Some inauguration into the 'fishing industry,' I mused.

However Frank managed to fire me with some

enthusiasm for the project and on a cold blustery March morning we set off for the shores of east Kintyre. It was a back-breaking experience, accompanied by an easterly wind which bit to the bone.

We spent our entire day's wages in the public bar of the Argyll Arms Hotel that evening and decided to leave whelk gathering to the professionals. Not that a lot of beer could be purchased for ten shillings! (50p) .

I hold a healthy respect for the permanent whelkers who are to be seen stooped about their business around the peninsula.

My late father, who was then manager of the local net factory, came to my rescue with two weeks' employment making helicopter slings for the army. As the only male worker amid twenty young maidens I found the experience most enjoyable.

I was ecstatic, though, when Ronnie finally announced that the boat was ready and we would be sailing in partnership with the **Seeker** (CN 49) under skipper James Rennie. It was with eager anticipation that I donned my heavy boots and oilskins for the first time.

From time to time throughout this publication I shall make reference to the various boats and skippers I have sailed with. The following list may be helpful to the reader.

Brighter Hope (CN 16) skipper Ronnie Brownie

Bonnie Lass (CN 115) skipper Ronnie Brownie
Girl Margaret (CN 158) skipper Andy Harrison
Alliance (CN 187) skippers William and Robert
  Gillies
Golden Fleece (CN 196) the author
Girl May (CN 240) skipper Andy Harrison
Peaceful Waters (CN 237) skipper Nigel McCrindle
Boy David (TT 78) skipper Colin Oman
Aquila (OB 99) skippers Cecil and Tommy Finn
Brighter Morn (CN 151) skippers Cecil and
  Tommy Finn
Strathisla (CN240) skippers Andy and Andrew
  Harrison Jnr
Atlas (CN 258) skippers Andy and Andrew
  Harrison Jnr
Nostaw (SN 48) skipper Alec Burnfield
Forards (B 300) skipper Fergie Hughes
Sceptre (OB 73) the author

The Coal Tar

CAMPBELTOWN, Argyll, lies at the head of the loch of that name which was immortalised in song by the Scots singer Andy Stewart. Situated almost at the end of the finger-like peninsula of Kintyre, it nestles below the majestic heather-clad slopes of Ben Ghuilean and Knockscalbert. Davaar Island lies protectively at the loch's entrance, making Campbeltown Harbour one of the safest on the Scottish west coast.

Despite a worrying hard core unemployment figure of some 15 per cent, there is an air of hope about the place and an excellent quality of life is enjoyed. The fishing industry, including ancillary workers, was at one time the town's principal employer. In its heyday 600 men followed the herring fishing in sailing skiffs. Today, however, there are only one pair of herring boats engaged in the fishery, the remainder of the fleet following the trawling method for prawns and white fish.

Whisky distilling was a major industry at the turn of this century, when 34 stills were in operation, with more than six million gallons of the 'cratur' in bond. Nowadays there are only two distilleries and a few bonded warehouses. Many of the opulent mansions which line the shores of the loch are known as 'whisky hooses', such was the prosperity of their owners.

There is a story often told about a small coaster, or 'puffer' making a passage up Campbeltown Loch in dense fog. A raw deckhand asked the old skipper which port they were approaching and he replied with a twinkle in his eye:

"Well I'm naw too sure, but by the smell o' it I wad say it was Campbeltown."

The local accent is a curious blend of broad Scots, Highland lilt, Lowland slang and a trace of the Irish brogue. Indeed, it is quite unique.

Townspeople lead an active social life within the various organisations in the burgh. In addition there are Chinese and Indian restaurants, cinema, bingo, swimming pool, discotheque, ceilidhs and dances. Incredibly, there are no fewer than 13 public houses serving a population (in the early 1990s) of 6,200.

Campbeltown is proud of its amateur football team, Pupils AFC, who climbed seven divisions in the Scottish Amateur League and are now perched in a firm position in the league's élite premier set up, narrowly missing the championship in season 1987/'88.

There are two fully-manned pipe bands and the gaelic choir has a strong reputation in Mod circles.

The area's most famous resident is the legendary Paul McCartney who owns two farms overlooking Machrihanish Bay and the Mull of Kintyre. It was in this peaceful setting that he composed the words and music of Britain's second best ever selling record, *Mull of Kintyre*. The Ceannloch Pipe Band, under Pipe-Major Tony Wilson, featured prominently on the disc.

The *Glasgow Herald* carried a report some winters ago about a BBC film unit stranded by snow on the Campbeltown-Tarbert road. The item concluded with a quote from the producer who said on his return to Glasgow that it was nice to get back to 'civilisation'. I don't see anything civilised about violence, robbery, muggings, hard drug-taking and the general wholesale crime that is so prevalent in our cities. Major crime is almost unknown in our little corner of Caledonia and the odd serious incident which has occurred has been at the hands of an 'outside mob'.

The trimmed-down Campbeltown fishing fleet consists of some 15 wooden and steel-built boats of lengths varying between 40 and 70 feet, the latter being the maximum allowed in the Firth of Clyde following legislation laid down in 1985.

They are driven by diesel engines of proven ability, including Gardner, Kelvin, Caterpillar and

Volvo, the power range being in the 110 h.p. to 450 h.p. bracket. Hydraulic cranes and winches assist greatly in the recovery of the gear.

The boats are equipped with the latest fish detection equipment and other electronic wizardry, including Decca navigator and video track plotter, radar, sonar, video colour echo sounder, paper recording echo sounder, and a host of radio equipment including CB. It is ironic that most of this gear is of Japanese manufacture despite the fact that Britain gave the world so many of the original ideas and models.

Romantic sounding names adorn the boats' bows and naming a vessel is always a matter for careful thought by parties concerned. A few examples which spring to mind are:–
Stella Maris (CN 158); **True Token** (CN 298); **Amazing Grace** (CN 289); **Brighter Morn** (CN 151); **Nova Spero** (CN 187); **Adoration** (CN 78).

Skippers are proud of their vessels, which are kept in pristine condition by extensive annual refit and a pleasure to the eye is the sight of a newly-painted boat steaming into the harbour.

At the risk of appearing biased, I would say that the flagship of the fleet for years was the 60-foot **Alliance** (CN 187), which was operated by my brothers, Robert being skipper. At 14 years old she was still immaculately varnished. Each spring the boat went back to the boatyard of her birth, Noble of Girvan, to be scraped bare before being coated with six applications of varnish, leaving her with a yacht-like finish. She was sold to proud Irish owners in 1989 when Robert and Willie bought the bigger **Nova Spero.**

The men who crew the boats have been known to other seafarers for generations as 'The Coal Tar', though I have been unable to find out why.

Unlike our counterparts in north east Scotland who have had to invest heavily in huge boats to combat the rigours of the North Sea, fishing from Campbeltown is carried on at a more leisurely pace, though the same rugged determination to succeed is very much in evidence.

There seems to be more of a 'family' atmosphere on the boats and the men mix well socially. The telling of little untruths or even downright lies over the radio by skippers intent on keeping secret a particularly lucrative fishing spot are always forgotten in port.

The Campbeltown fishermen's annual dinner dance is always a well-attended gala occasion. In addition, the branch contributes generous amounts to various local charities.

Nomadic by nature in days gone by when herring fishing was all important to the fleet's economy, skippers now concentrate mainly on day trips for prawns and white fish during the winter months, landing each night at Campbeltown. Week-long trips to grounds in the Sound of Jura and the Minch are made in spring and summer. Only two boats, the **Nova Spero** and **Brighter Morn** participate in herring-fishing using the pair-trawl method.

A sore point among the Campbeltown fishermen for years has been the continued poor prices, in comparison with other ports, for white fish. One has only to read market reports from other areas to understand why. Some blame road distance, others the lack of volume of landings. Whatever the reason, the situation seems set to go on as it is.

The local system of paying a share fisherman is one of the fairest I know.

At the end of each week, the firm of CMC Fishselling prepares a sales sheet which itemises each item of expenditure such as fuel, food, NHI contributions and so on. This sum is deducted from the total grossing, the balance of which is divided equally between boat and crew.

For example, if a boat carries a crew of four and the sum to be divided after expenses is £1,600, each man receives £200. The remaing £800 goes to the skipper-owner to meet maintenance costs and the upkeep of fishing gear.

Needless to say, wages can vary wildly from week to week, depending on circumstances. A 'bonanza' wage often draws comments from outsiders, but they never seem to hear about the slack period caused by scarcity, bad weather or perhaps a mechanical break-down.

As is usual in fishing ports, there is a watering hole favoured by men of the sea and in this case it is the Feathers Inn in the town's Cross Street, where many of the fishermen gather of a Saturday to discuss the week's results.

Mine host at the Feathers, the ebullient Jim Greene, has often said that after listening to the Coal Tar's stimulant-fired repartee for so long he could easily take a boat to the sea himself and could open a shop to sell the fish and prawns netted in his premises at weekends.

Drinking, incidentally, is heavily frowned upon on board and is confined to shore leave.

We are joined periodically by 'strangers', possibly attracted by the natural beauty of the district or harbouring notions of an adventurous life in fishing. These men are always made welcome, but with a few rare exceptions they usually retreat somewhat disillusioned. I have seen engineers, policemen, ex-servicemen, and tradesmen all come and go. A prominent Scottish daily newspaper reporter even reached the stage of negotiating to buy a boat before deciding to return to a desk-bound job and the familiar smell of newsprint.

Accommodation aboard the boats is warm and comfortable. Padded locker seating is arranged around a central cabin table and most boats have six roomy bunks, Some have hot water units and sinks and have had refrigerators and television installed. Cooking is done on modern calor gas stoves – a far cry from the days of the 'Jack Tar' coal fire and primus stove.

While the boats could almost be called floating houses, there is a basic amenity which is lacking in the vast majority of cases and that is the provision of a flush toilet.

Emptying the bladder is a simple case of adding slightly to the level of the ocean but other business is accomplished by a visit to 'the can,' a luxuriously appointed discarded five gallon oil drum. Careful removal of the top with hammer and chisel, followed by the application of a length of split rubber hose around the rim and the adding of rope handles completes the fabrication of the portaloo. On half filling with sea water, the 'can' may be used at any discreet part of the boat.

It must seem barbaric to people ashore but using the 'can' comes as second nature to us.

One old local skipper, now retired, steadfastly refused to use the 'can' in privacy and could often be seen sitting quite unabashed on his throne by the side of the wheelhouse, puffing his pipe contentedly.

When fishing away from home, inter-boat visits are made and the tobacco filled cabins overflow with men aboard for the 'yarn'. The talk usually veers away from fishing and one such evening was in full swing at the Isle of Gigha anchorage when the subject of holidays came up.

Skipper Cecil Finn told how on a beach at Tenerife he was accosted by three elderly matrons who vociferously demanded his autograph, insisting he was Amos the barman in the television series *Emmerdale Farm.* They refused to leave him in peace until he consented to sign, thus committing the only act of forgery of his life! It wasn't until that night that it struck me just how similar the two men are in appearance. I have had many hours of entertainment at these ceilidhs afloat.

Despite my lean angular frame I have a Herculean appetite while at sea, a trait shared by nearly every fisherman I know. Eating aboard, therefore, is a joyous experience to behold. Most fishermen are good cooks as tradition decrees that young men joining the industry are given this position and, through trial and error patiently endured by older hands, a degree of proficiency is attained. I have sailed with a lot of fine cooks who are capable of producing the most appetising dishes out of basic ingredients.

Two of the best cooks I have encountered during the past couple of decades are Henry O'Hara and Hamish Wareham, both from Campbeltown.

Henry, now working for the Government at the Machrihanish RAF Station was cook on the **Girl Margaret.** It was from him that I learned any culinary skills I possess. What amazed me about the

Skipper Cecil Finn in 'Amos' of *Emmerdale Farm* pose, photographed aboard
Aquila" in 1983

methodical Henry was that even in the confined
space of the boat's forward accommodation he
could prepare a magnificent dinner in a quiet
unobtrusive manner with the rest of the crew barely

noticing what was going on. Henry's meals could grace any restaurant table.

Hamish is still at sea as 'chef' on the latest **Brighter Morn,** with skipper Tommy Finn. This modern vessel has excellent mess deck facilities which include all-electric fridge, toaster, kettle, cooker and deep freeze. Hamish is in his element amid such luxuries and his 'pièce de résistance' is fish and chips.

I have eaten fish suppers in places the length and breadth of Britain and have yet to find anything to compare with Hamish's haddock and chips. It must be remembered that as well as providing meals for ravenous deckies, cooks also have to carry out normal duties on the boat and receive no extra wages. A good cook is a valued member of any crew and many a skipper regards such as being the most important man on the boat.

Gargantuan fried breakfasts and huge dinners are commonplace and would give any dietician a nightmare. Because of the irregular hours we work, especially at the herring fishing, I have sampled such delicacies as fish and chips or gigot chop casserole at breakfast time, the thought of which would undoubtedly put the nine to five man off his lightly boiled egg and toast.

A typical sea breakfast could consist of sausage, bacon, eggs, mushrooms, beans, black pudding, potato scones and two half pint mugs of tea. I've seen two loaves disappear at a breakfast sitting of four men.

Normal dinner menus feature steaks, roast beef, or perhaps two chickens accompanied by two veg and a veritable mountain of potatoes. There is usually a pot of home made soup sitting on the cooker, ready for consumption at any time. And, of course, the kettle is never off the boil.

Contrary to common belief, we do not eat fish until it comes out of our ears, though it does constitute part of our diet. Could it be that the longevity of the Campbeltown fishermen of two generations ago was attributable to the fact that fish was their staple diet? One also has only to look at the healthy fish-eating Icelanders to cause us to ask ourselves if we eat enough fish. Icelanders and Eskimos share the lowest heart disease rate in the world.

A local GP came to sea with us on a fishing trip on the **Alliance** and was astonished at the amount of food which was consumed. He went ashore leaving a friendly warning that if any of the crew consulted him complaining of a stomach disorder a large dose of castor oil would be prescribed.

The weather dictates to a great extent the planning of fishing operations and the shipping forecast is awaited eagerly each day. Gale force winds in winter often mean a suspension of fishing and a visit to the 'buroo' but it is carried on in conditions which could almost qualify as gale force.

Flat calms are rare in the winter months and it

can be a most uncomfortable and hazardous experience attempting to work normally on an open deck when the boat is rolling like a barrel during a blow. The cold brings its miseries too and I shiver involuntarily when I think of days spent gutting fish or tailing prawns while trying to decide which was the lesser of two evils – freezing hands or the uncontrollable stream from the nasal region. One of the most depressing ways to start a day is to shoot a trawl on a grey December dawn which has been heralded by a strong south-easterly breeze and lashing sleet. Despite the fact that some boats have two radar sets, sea fog and blinding snow still give me a haunting feeling of helplessness at not being able to see past the bow with the naked eye.

We are often drenched by flying spray, even when wrapped up in protective clothing, and the romantic image of a fisherman in glistening oilskins probably means that he is soaked to the skin with condensation inside the garments. The dampness too, always seems to find its way into the accommodation area where the smell of drying woollen jumpers and socks in the confined space can be most offensive. And if someone happens to have smelly feet …

Sometimes at such times I yearn for town pavements and ask myself what I am doing there. The feeling soon passes.

I have often been asked to describe the worst day I spent at sea and there is no doubt in my mind that this was during a passage from the Isle of Gigha to Campbeltown in October 1975, aboard the **Alliance.**

A girning north-westerly breeze was showing signs of increasing on our departure from Gigha but we calculated that the notorious Mull of Kintyre would be rounded before any real weight came into the wind. However, midway between Machrihanish Bay and the Mull Lighthouse, the 'breeze' rose to a screaming fury and we were well and truly caught. To turn back would have meant a shoulder-on battering for hours and since we were so close to the Mull, where seven different tidal races meet, it was decided to press on.

On arrival below the lighthouse we discovered that the motion had risen to an alarming height and, coupled with the confusion of the tide, had turned the area into a boiling cauldron. There was a constant danger of the boat broaching-to (ie being thrown beam on to the sea by the following waves). Lumps of green water broke over the bow and stern simultaneously and I maintain to this day that it was the vast experience and superb seamanship displayed by my father which enabled us to reach the safe lee of the Sound of Sanda, where we noted that the heavy trawl net had been washed from the stern to a position forward of the wheelhouse.

A close second to this battle with the elements took place in a position some 20 miles west of Tory Island, Co. Donegal, where we were trawling with the **Brighter Morn** in March 1989.

No Campbeltown boat had hitherto ventured as far out into the Atlantic but we felt that the sturdily-built boat was suitable for such waters.

Apart from annoying damage to the nets caused by the wreckage of sunken wartime merchantmen – we were fishing bang on the North Atlantic convoy route – good hauls of codling, haddock and flatfish were being made.

The perpetual swell in these waters caused the boat to roll constantly. Caution while shooting and hauling the gear was exercised and while life was uncomfortable to say the least, we managed to put in a good two days and two nights fishing in company with several much larger ships including two big Spanish trawlers.

The sea area Malin forecast for the third morning gave south-south-east force four/five. However, the wind backed to south-east and a force eight sprang up from nowhere, with resultant crests breaking on top of 20 foot rollers. The boat began to toss like a cork and heaving the gear was a slow and arduous process. When the net was safely aboard it was decided there was only one course of action open to us and that was to dodge in for the lee of the Irish land. To turn and run before the sea would only have pushed us further out into the Atlantic towards the edge of the Continental Shelf.

Tommy by this time was pretty well all-in, having spent some 18 hours in the wheelhouse. As mate, I was detailed to take the watch accompanied by crewmen Stewart Anderson, and Tommy retired below.

The following hours were the longest of my life, as the boat pitched and rolled violently. To even contemplate making coffee to sustain us was out of the question. Thankfully the **Brighter Morn** is equipped with automatic pilot which meant I could make course alterations quickly. I tried to 'meet' the sea as much as possible by altering to starboard then to port in the trough of the waves to avoid the beam on effect of the sea.

Far away in the sanctuary of the Firth of Clyde, brother Robert in the **Alliance** was in constant touch by 400 watt radio and I kept him informed of our progress.

Six hours, 18 zig-zag miles and 30 cigarettes later we were finally able to turn the **Brighter Morn** stern on to the now greatly reduced motion and head for the safety of Greencastle, Co. Donegal.

I said at the time and I shall say it again here that the next time I see Tory Island will be from the deck of the QE2 or something similar.

In direct comparison, fishing in the summer is a most pleasurable occupation. The tranquillity of a soft July dawn has to be experienced to be believed.

We usually fish for herring at this time, often at night, and are frequently close inshore where the delightfully pungent fragrance of blooming heather and ferns, intermingled with pines and other flora wafts lazily over the boat. It is as if the heavy night air holds these unforgettable aromas in suspension.

The eerie call of a lonely curlew or other nocturnal birds of prey can often be heard echoing across the calm inky blue waters.

For the herring fisherman this is also the time of long daylight hours spent sometimes at some remote pier, presenting the opportunity of a swim in crystal clear waters or a ramble through some of the finest scenery in Britain, caught up in a time trap.

Porpoises swim along with the boats for miles in summer and I never fail to marvel at their friendliness and amazing agility.

Campbeltown fishermen are used to seeing pairs of porpoises in the Clyde and hardly give them a second glance. The interest of the **Brighter Morn's** crew, however, was aroused considerably one day in May 1989 whilst fishing off Tiree when a huge school appeared alongside.

The lively, intelligent mammals surrounded the boat in a diving, thrashing mass and entertained us for about an hour before swimming off in a north-westerly direction. We counted at least 200. The likely explanation is that they were on a migratory path and stopped off for a bit of fun on the way.

Basking sharks are much in evidence, too, during this period and though they can cause extensive damage to herring gear if netted, there is something majestic about their slow, deliberate movements on the surface.

On one fabulous occasion in July 1985 we counted 70 basking sharks in a small area of Kilbrannan Sound. Not even the oldest of retired Campbeltown fishermen could remember seeing sharks in such numbers and the phenomenon is largely unexplained.

Prawn fishermen spend the gloriously calm summer days lying on deck between hauls, their half-naked torsos soaking up the warming rays as the boat meanders through a sea of painted blue glass.

To watch a crimson sun sink slowly behind the emerald jewels of the Inner Hebrides gives one a feeling of well-being. A man could give up wife and promotion to be part of the scene, light years away from Wolverhampton.

Almost every nook and cranny on the coasts of Kintyre and Arran has a name. Some appear on official charts but many were provided by the Coal Tar of old.

I was familiar with most of the better-known landmarks through my youthful excursions to sea but I have added to my mental store of place names, courtesy of skipper Cecil Finn. He has an intimate knowledge of the shore gleaned through many years of seine-netting for white fish and is only too happy to pass on information, accompanied by historical background where possible, to willing ears.

I have stood beside him on many a quiet summer evening, skirting magical places like Imachar (Eemachur); Tandergay (Thunderguy); Crossaig Skiervuile (Scarevoolie); Ronascarbh (Ronnascariff); The Rhu (Roo); Sunadale (Soonadill); to name but a few.

Mary McEwen's is a small islet on the north side of Saddell Bay which lies testimony to a nurse of that name who ended her young life there after being spurned by a man she sorely loved. The Longstonedyke (pronounced quickly as Longstindake) is a snaking drystone wall which runs from the top of one of Arran's hills to almost sea level.

The Green Patch, so appropriately named, is a curiously isolated square of lush pasture set amid the barren rock and rugged slopes of the Brown Head, at the south end of Arran. And further along the Arran shore to the eastward is a small bay which owes its name to the well-known netting firm of Bridport Gundry. So many ring nets were either lost or badly torn on its rock strewn bottom that it soon became known as Gundry's Bight.

The Picture Cave on the south face of Davaar Island overlooks another famous herring area known as the Lowdon. Anyone visiting Campbeltown should endeavour to see the cave which contains one of the world's most unusual paintings of Jesus.

In 1887 an impoverished local artist, Archibald McKinnon, had a vision in which he saw Christ on the cross portrayed not on canvas but on a cave wall. Daily for six weeks McKinnon made his way to the island cave via the Dhorlin, a tidal sandbank which separates Davaar from the mainland.

He completed his task using brushes tied to walking sticks in place of scaffolding and his secret remained with him until a group of young fishermen on an evening trip to the island went into the cave. As their eyes grew accustomed to the light a huge picture of the Crucifixion appeared before them and in a state of terror they made off for the town, where the news quickly spread. It was not until several years later that the mystery was solved.

The painting has been re-touched three times and is still in good condition.

Nature has also played a part in the naming of landmarks, one of the most obvious being the Sleeping Warrior, a formation of hills and peaks on Arran which bear an uncanny resemblance to a soldier who has fallen in battle. The 'warrior' can be viewed from both Kilbrannan Sound and Inchmarnock Water and Mother Nature has even given him buttons on his greatcoat. The cliff face at a point between Pladda Island and the Bennan Head on Arran has been hewed by the elements through aeons to be left with an outline which is the

perfect facsimile of a Clydesdale horse. The fact
that a narrow cascading waterfall spills like foaming
beer from its rear end caused this spot to be
dubbed 'The Pissing Mare' by the Coal Tar.

My mother asked me one evening where we
had spent the day fishing and without thought I
replied:

"Oh, the pissing mare".

"Kindly refer to that place as the watering
horse in front of your mother," my father
instructed me later.

As well as being adept at naming places, the
Coal Tar have always bestowed nicknames on each
other and are usually addressed as such. Some of
my contemporaries known in this way are Bomber
(John Brown); Soda (John Meenan); Bun (Robert
McGeachy); Nuclar (Andrew Robertson); Collie
(Ian McAulay); Big Fee (John McPhee); Sna (Angus
McEachran); Keka (Stuart Anderson); Rancher
(Duncan Lang). I have not escaped either, thanks to
a chance remark by my brother Robert (Trapper)
which was immediately seized upon by others.

On a whim I decided to grow a moustache
and through either laziness or a vain desire to
prove masculinity I allowed it to expand until it had
reached Mexican proportions. Trapper thought I
bore a slight resemblance to an old salt we can just
remember and who was nicknamed Doosan.
Apparently this man was a worshipper of the god
Bacchus and while I enjoy a drink like lots of my

fishing friends I don't share Doosan's one time enthusiasm for consuming wine of a dubious vintage in vast quantities.

I have accepted the 'handle' philosophically but secretly hope that if I continue to ignore it it will disappear into the mists of time.

No publication about Campbeltown fishing would be complete without reference being made to the now quite famous Campbeltown Shipyard Limited, arguably the finest builders of steel fishing boats in the UK.

Known to the Coal Tar as 'the yerd', the company has gone from strength to strength from humble beginnings in the early seventies, and now turns out 87-foot boats which cost well in excess of one million pounds. Built on the site of a derelict shipyard which closed during the depression, the yard's first completion was, appropriately, for local skipper James McDonald. She was the 50-foot transom sterned trawler **Crimson Arrow** (CN 30). Much interest was aroused throughout Scotland and a string of similar vessels followed over the next two years.

The yard's big break came, however, when the leading Scottish seine-net skipper William Campbell MBE, of Elgin, ordered an 80-footer. The launching of the **Argosy** (INS 79) in 1972 marked the beginning of an outstanding run of success for the yard and nearly 100 boats have been built to date, two of which have gone to the Faroe Islands.

The Campbeltown boats, apart from being constructed to a degree of excellence which is second to none, have tremendous sea-keeping qualities which enable skippers to keep on fishing while others lie-to in bad weather, and record landings are constantly being made.

Because of the huge amount of capital involved in the building of these ships, such a venture is outwith the reach of the Campbeltown men but they are nevertheless proud to be associated with the yard.

It was with delight that everyone connected with local fishing heard that the yard's managing director, Leslie Howarth, had been awarded the OBE in the 1987 New Year's Honours List.

The Silver Darlings

HERRING ring-netting, now completely discontinued in the Clyde, was showing signs of dying out when I first became a fisherman and I was pleased to have been able to take part during the final years.

The advent of pair-trawling by powerful boats towing huge nets meant that the ringers just could not compete and tradition had to make way for the march of progress, despite rigorous opposition by ring-net men, in particular the Carradale branch of the Clyde Fishermen's Association.

Ring-netting was practised by Campbeltown fishermen for generations and though the method basically remained unchanged, nets and boats increased in size and nylon eventually substituted cotton.

The boats, each carrying a net on the port quarter, operated during darkness in pairs and were crewed by five men and a boy. When a shoal of herring was detected, the net was shot in a wide semi-circle. The neighbour boat picked up the end,

Peaceful Carradale Harbour in the early 1970s

which was identified by a 'winkie' – a buoyant light attached to a rope extension from the end of the netting. Both vessels then towed the gear slowly through the water for a few minutes before turning towards each other. When this operation was completed, the crew of the neighbour boat jumped aboard with the end and hauling by hand commenced.

It is interesting to note that the young cook had always the hardest task of hauling the hard surface rope (backrope) to which the corks were attached. While the net was being hauled the neighbour boat, in a right angle position, kept a gentle strain on the towline, thus keeping the other vessel clear of the gear.

The herring were removed from the net when alongside by a brailer, which was just like a massive butterfly net, the tail of which was winched on board.

Before the days of echo sounders, shoals of herring were sometimes found by the use of the 'wire'. This was a long length of piano-thin wire, the end of which held a lead weight, and was towed slowly through the water. Experienced hands could tell when the wire came into contact with herring, rather than other fish. Another way of detecting the silver darlings was by crewmen looking over the stem of the boat at the 'burning', a magnificent show of phosphorescence caused by the boat churning through countless millions of microscopic organisms and plankton. Herring could easily be identified in the burning and many a fine ring was made in this way.

From the early days of open skiffs the boats gradually became more sophisticated with engines being installed and covered accommodation provided. Indeed, a Campbeltown man, the late Robert Robertson, is credited with being instrumental in pioneering much of the modern day ring-net fishing using advanced design ideas. He was involved in six herring boats and was the Clyde's most successful fisherman of his era – the 1930s

Since the largest modern ring-net could only

reach a depth of 15 fathoms, even with the
assistance of a bottom rope fitted with lead weights,
the method was at its most deadly on the
shorehead, where the net came into contact with
the bottom. Through this, many fishermen became
intimate with the nature of the seabed, knowledge
which was to prove invaluable as other methods of
fishing opened up.

The most advanced ring-netters, the last of
which were built in the sixties and early seventies,
were between 50 and 63 feet long. Invariably
wooden-built, with cruiser sterns, these boats had
sleek lines and were usually varnished. The
wheelhouse was a small box-like construction,
designed so as to catch the minimum amount of
wind while fishing.

Accommodation for six men was set forward
and a large fish room separated the forecastle from
the engine room, which housed diesels of anything
up to 350 h.p.

Ring-netting in the Clyde was only really
successful at night, and the amount of hours spent
at sea in the summer were minimal. It was not
unusual to leave Carradale at 11 p.m. and return at
4 a.m.

It was a different story in winter, when boats
could be at sea from four o'clock in the afternoon
until eight the following morning. If things were
slack, though, the fleet sometimes anchored for a
few hours. My first berth at the herring and,

indeed, the fishing, was with Ronnie on the **Brighter Hope** and the transition from office-worker to 'hairy wullie' was made with surprising ease. Apart from a few blisters on my hands, thanks to the back-rope, there were no real problems. It did strike me though, that instead of being a passenger as I had been so often in the past, I was now part of the crew, being paid the same wages and therefore expected to do the same work. My first wage was £37.

These halcyon days at the ring-netting have given me some of my fondest memories of the fishing, perhaps because it was summer and the weather was perfect. Catches were steady, not only at the fishing, but along the promenades of Rothesay or Largs. Or perhaps the pier head at Lochranza, Brodick or Tarbert. There seemed to be an abundance of young members of the opposite sex during that vintage year.

Our boat was lying at the little pier at Carrick Castle, Loch Goil, on one of these idyllic occasions when a smart yacht moored alongside. Trying to impress a fair young lassie aboard the pleasure craft, I scaled the walls of the ancient crumbling fortress that stands on the pier. Midway up, I was overcome by a severe attack of vertigo and only much cajoling and advice from my mates got me down safely, to the extreme merriment of one yellow-wellied young lady.

Since at that time there was no swimming pool

in Campbeltown, an important part of the weekly fishing kit was swimming gear, as the boats often berthed at the classier Clyde resorts equipped with such amenities and it was no uncommon sight to see seven or eight young Campbeltown fishermen floundering in a pool along with the holidaymakers.

Spirits were usually high, especially if the neighbour boat was away to the Ayr market with herring and one such day found us in the pool at Rothesay. There was a kiddies' chute at one end of the baths and, despite warning notices to the contrary, my brother Willie decided to do a 'belly flopper' into the water. Arms straight ahead, head down, his 14 stone frame sliced into the water like a knife and only stopped when his head hit the tiled bottom.

Fortunately, he received only a small cut, but it was a red-faced band of fisher lads who made their way back to the boats following a severe reprimand from the pool attendant.

Filming of a special St Andrews day programme featuring Andy Stewart was in progress at Lochranza, where we moored one afternoon.

The television producer decided he would like the boat included in the scene, which was to feature Andy as a 'drunken sailor' falling off the pier.

Complicated setting up of the equipment followed and at last everything was ready to roll.

At a crucial point in the shooting, with Andy

in the act of plunging headlong into the Firth of Clyde, someone on the boat decided to fire up the galley stove using a quantity of diesel oil. The resultant pall of thick black smoke which shot out of the chimney was not appreciated by the film crew, or Andy, as the scene had to be done again, giving the star his second soaking of the day.

However, we were forgiven and spent an hour or so chatting to the celebrated cast.

Ringing in summer was not all a bed of roses. The bane of a herring fisherman's life during the hot months are the red stinging jellyfish known as 'scouders' which are at their most prolific in warm weather. I have been stung on the face, arms, nose and in the eyes.

There are no magic creams or potions to alleviate the pain and only a margin of relief can be obtained by holding the affected part as close to intense heat as possible, such as a cabin fire. This, understandably, is most uncomfortable. Even touching a net which has been ashore for weeks can result in a dry sting.

The largest amount of scouders I have ever seen was at the mouth of Loch Striven in the Kyles of Bute. Ronnie picked up a nice mark on the echo sounder and the net was duly shot. We looked in disbelief when the net was hauled to reveal a solid mass of the blighters. Older crewman reckoned there was the bulk of 250 baskets in the net and that they had shown up on the sounder just as a herring shoal would.

Another scourge of the ring-net men was a 'rolling'. This happened usually during a strong tide, in shallow water where the seabed was littered with shells. The shells entangled themselves in the netting, which rolled itself round the leaded sole rope. Queen scallops, with their bi-valve shells, caused the worst rolling and I have seen one as thick as a man's body, which took 11 hours to unravel.

Despite these little nuisances, however, the ringing will always hold a special place in my heart, and it is a sad fact that I shall never again be able to participate in the fishery, which nowadays is referred to as the 'Galilean method'.

The Wombles

THE greater part of my fishing career has been spent in pursuit of prawns using the trawling method.

Almost every fisherman I know would far rather be involved in other types of fishing, but prawning is vital to the economy of the Campbeltown fleet and remains its mainstay.

It is not the actual catching of the prawns that most men dislike, but the long, weary hours spent preparing them for market when fishing is heavy. Prawns of a certain length can be kept intact but the vast majority must be 'tailed', that is the separation of the head from the body. Relentless trawling over the past 30 years has meant a considerable reduction in size of the species and small prawns have been dubbed variously as 'beetles', 'Indian corn', 'Ruskoline', 'lentils' and, goodness knows why, 'wombles'.

Prawn trawling began in Campbeltown in the late 1950s. Before prawns became popular with the gourmet, they were regarded with disgust by seine-net fishermen, who shovelled them back over the side after retaining haddock, whiting, etc. from the catch.

However, it soon became an extremely viable fishery and eventually overtook herring ring-netting as the main method employed, with very little conversion needed to the boats

Prawn grounds are extensive, stretching from the Clyde to the North Minch on the west coast. The Whitehaven area and the Irish Sea between Ulster and the Isle of Man are other lucrative areas.

The North Sea, too, has big areas of good prawn territory. Many of the Clyde boats follow the fishing on a seasonal basis and are usually based in Mallaig in early summer.

Indeed, it was the Campbeltown skipper Andy Harrison who pioneered the rockhopper fishing around the islands and lochs on the south end of Skye, landing some remarkable shots of large prawns in the early 80s. Needless to say, the quality has gone downhill since, due to intense effort by many. Prawns are caught in nets designed to 'dig' slightly on the muddy seabed to give a scooping effect. They are held open by steel trawl doors, or boards, which come along the bottom ahead of the net. During strong tides the prawns retreat into mudholes, with a substantially adverse effect on fishing.

To combat this, robust trawls specially made for working the mud surrounding rock on the seabed in shallow water are used. These nets are fitted with 'rockhoppers', 14" rubber discs which, in theory, are supposed to bounce over the hard ground, thus lifting the net 'up and over'. Unfortunately this is not always the case and many an hour has been spent mending a badly torn net.

In the case of the ordinary prawn trawl, too much dig causes the net to 'mud-up', or fill up with mud balls known as spuds such is their likeness to potatoes. Towing the gear too hard, on the other hand, can result in a 'flyer', where the net has had little contact with the bottom, thereby producing a blank tow.

Early morning and late evening in spring and summer are best prawn fishing times.

During periods of heavy fishing when conditions are just right, it is impossible to clear the deck in time for the next haul coming aboard. For example, if a tow produces 15 stone of tails counting 80 to the pound no fewer than 16,800 prawns will have to be tailed in three hours. Most boats only have two deckhands nowadays.

As one shipmate once remarked to me at the tailing bench: "This is a great job when you don't get any".

I remember vividly the time the **Alliance's** crew sat down to Monday's dinner at 2.30 a.m. on Tuesday after a particularly successful day on the Sound of Jura grounds. And I don't suppose the **Girl May's** cook, Malcolm Wilkinson, was all that

amused when my head collapsed with exhaustion
into a plate of succulent scrambled eggs on toast he
had produced for breakfast. That was the time we
turned in at 2.50 a.m. and resumed fishing at 3.30
a.m. What fun! Working with such bulk causes
other problems such as aching backs and 'prawn
wrist'. The perpetual screwing motion with the
hands can lead to a wrist swelling to alarming
proportions.

In the early days of prawn fishing, crewmen
sat on the boat's low rail and tailed the prawns off a
'table' – usually just a square of marine plywood.
Completely exposed to wind and sea, conditions
were pretty well intolerable and even gloved hands
were often frozen into numbness. These days, most
boats have shelter decks fitted to cut out the wind
chill factor and the men stand around a properly
constructed bench to sort the catch.

It is a different story, of course, when things
are slack. As I write, the result of a four-hour tow is
lying in state on deck in one box. It is at times like
this that the 'nonsense' and the wind-ups take over
on the radio. I suppose it is one way of relieving the
inevitable boredom which occurs in the
wheelhouse.

Crewmen, too, pass the time getting up to all
sorts of tricks. One Donald Lawson, of
Campbeltown, is noted for his exploits.

On one occasion he switched the labels around
on a variety of tinned goods, causing the cook much

consternation as he gallantly attempted to make meals.

Another time Donald stuffed an egg into the rear cavity of a chicken which was to be cooked for dinner. Some of the ensuing comments were priceless.

Twin rig trawling, the towing of two nets, was taken up by some boats about four years ago to increase catches, expecially at strong tide time. Many vessels are now fitted out for this method, but there is opposition by several fishermen's organisations. In fact the fleets are divided on the issue and a ban on the method is being called for from various quarters. The prawn market has been sticky in recent times and it is claimed that increased landings from large twin rig boats is a contributory factor.

Many weird and wonderful things are brought up from the bottom in prawn nets, some pleasantly surprising, others offensive.

One Irish skipper fishing near Ailsa Craig became the owner of a 500 c.c. motor cycle. It had not been in the water for long and was restored fully. It is astonishing to record that, almost 50 years after hostilities ended, wartime mines, bombs and torpedoes still turn up. A high percentage of these devices are still live and have to be dealt with by the Faslane Bomb Disposal Unit.

I think the funniest item I have ever seen dropping out of a codend was a lavatory pan, in

perfect condition and complete with seat. I was with
Nigel in the **Peaceful Waters** when this was netted
in the Whiting Bay area on the east side of Arran.
One of the lads sat on it while tailing on the way
back to Campbeltown.

The late William Colville, better known as 'The Count', called on me during my *Courier* days to show me a top set of false teeth he had discovered in the belly of a big cod while fishing with skipper Eddie Lafferty on the **Kirsteen Anne** (CN 263).

The barbarity of the practice of drowning unwanted pups was brought home fully to me after we had hauled in Kilbrannan Sound one day. Investigating a neatly tied sack which had come aboard with the prawns, I found it contained four days-old collie pups, possibly discarded by a farmer. I was annoyed for days about it.

The most offensive unwanted catch I was involved in was a seal in the latter stages of decomposition, which we netted on the **Girl May** off Islay. The smell was indescribable. The waters just off the high cliffs of the Sleat Peninsula on Skye have yielded dead sheep several times, due probably to the animals losing their footing on the precipitous headland.

Things were extremely quiet aboard the **Nostaw** on a late summer afternoon of complete calm and bright sunshine as we trawled our way towards Gigha. It was landing night, not that there was much to put ashore due to viciously strong tides. In fact, Skipper Alec Burnfield and I had already decided that we were merely passing the time until we were due to make for Tayinloan, Kintyre, where the lorry for Campbeltown was due.

Hauling time duly arrived and our worst fears were realised when the net floated up to the surface – an obvious sign of a empty codend. Sure enough, when the bag was opened, the contents would not have filled a basket. However, there were two items on the deck which caused us to look incredulously at one another – a large lobster and a bottle of Grouse whisky.

No one would believe Alec when he reported the haul on the radio and we spent that night at Gigha making the rounds of the boats with our prize catch to prove it.

Tows in lochs which are recognised anchorages sometimes produce old earthenware vessels and wine bottles – some of which can be valuable – discarded from early pleasure steamers and yachts.

Many boats from other ports use Campbeltown as a landing base, principally men from Portavogie, Northern Ireland and Ayrshire. Through this I have made many lifetime friends who are highly thought of. My oldest buddie is Davy McClements, an Irishman of repute, who owns and skippers the **Ilene** (B 152), Robbie McVey of the **Daystar** (B 131), can almost qualify for local citizenship such is his fondness for 'the wee toon'. Another chum is Robert Murray, of the **Harvest Reaper**.

My Ayrshire mates include Lorimer 'Noddy' Gibson, Hugh Currie, Howard McCrindle, Hugh

'Junior' McPhee, Ian 'Poogie' Anderson and Donald 'Sugar' McCrindle, to name but a few.

As I think about the number of men and boats involved in the prawn fishery, it is brought home just how important the humble prawn is. Portavogie alone boasts a fleet of 100 vessels, though only a part of that number fishes in the firth, and the combined fleets of Kintyre and Ayrshire number something like 120.

Perhaps it is just as well that prawns breed prolifically!

Bent to the task. Sorting prawns with crewman Danny Taylor on the **Sceptre** *1990.*

Queenie Fever

SEASONAL Queen Scallop fishing was at fever pitch during my first few years as a fisherman and I enjoyed this fishery immensely, principally because it was practised in sheltered inshore waters and did not involve 'rolling to the numbers' as prawn trawling so often did, during the September to December period.

The queenies, or crechans, to give them their local name, had been nestling quite happily on the sea bed through the ages and nobody was interested in catching them, let alone buying them. That was until around 1969 when they suddenly became the 'in-thing' in fashionable American restaurants.

At first a few boats supplied the limited market and caught the queenies using modified clam dredges, but as demand grew the Campbeltown netmaking firms of Flaws and Shaw and Bridport-Gundry Ltd introduced specially designed trawls which proved to be more effective.

Before long, almost every boat in the

Campbeltown, Carradale and Tarbert fleets was pursuing the queenies and results were so spectacular that a quota system had to be introduced. Four processing plants were in operation in Campbeltown alone, providing much needed employment for many. They were Kilbrannan Seafoods, Neptune Seafoods, Davaar Seafoods and Gilchrist Seafoods. Individual landings of 100 eight stone bags was a common daily occurrence for many boats at the height of the fishery, which centred originally along the Kintyre and Arran coasts.

As the stocks gradually thinned out, the Campbeltown men spread their wings to the Ayrshire coast and more thick beds were discovered. Intensified fishing led to a drastic reduction in stocks and while there is still a limited autumn fishery, the landings of the early 70s are unlikely to be seen again.

Only two processing plants, McConnachie Seafoods and Mull of Kintyre Seafoods remain in Campbeltown today.

The queenie trawl is very similar in appearance to a prawn net, but is made up of heavy duty double twined netting to prevent chafing on the firm sandy bottom the species frequent. Attached to the ground rope are a number of pressurised rubber wheels of 14" diameter called bobbins, designed to enable the trawl to travel over rough and rocky ground without damage.

Although the net is much smaller than the prawn trawl, the 'mouth' has to have a high opening as the queenies can jump an astonishing nine feet from the sea bed when disturbed.

Protection for the underside of the cod end was a problem faced by the early queenie fishermen.

Constant contact with the bottom caused by the weight of the shells caused never ending damage to the bag and many different ideas were put to the test. These included jute sacking, canvas, more netting, and one enterprising skipper even fell out with his wife when he disappeared to the boat with a piece of stair carpeting which he attached to his cod end.

When someone suggested using the hides from slaughtered cattle the idea was laughed to scorn, but the shoe was on the other foot when the theory went on trial and resulted in a fortnight's damage-free fishing. And all for the price of £3. The general stampede for hides which followed meant that an order had to be placed at the Glasgow Abattoir. As orders became heavier, the price crept up to £15, but it was still money well spent.

The hides had two distinct disadvantages, and both had nothing whatever to do with actual fishing. First, before they left the city by lorry, they were liberally coated with coarse salt and fishermen had to endure the stinging pain in their ever present hand cuts while fixing them to the trawl.

That was really nothing compared to the feeling experienced by nearly every deckie who had the unpleasant job of shooting the trawl first thing on a Monday morning. The smell of a partly used hide which was 'down to the skin' and had lain on the stern since Friday, coupled with the usual 'morning after' feeling, resulted in many a breakfast finding a watery grave. Hides have now been replaced with sections of a tough new type of conveyor belt.

Coming fast on the hard bottom at queenie fishing is an occupational hazard and therefore tows are of a short duration, usually about one hour. Fastners often result in the net coming up in a tangled mess which takes hours to clear.

I remember one day at Innellan in the River Clyde we snagged on a sunken mooring buoy and when the net came up it was completely inside out, just as a sock would look on removal from the foot. We could do nothing else but make for Rothesay and haul the whole lot on to the pier, where the rig was stripped of all the different bits and pieces and put back together again. These situations are known as 'hanks'.

Another bugbear at this method is the catching of huge boulders. If a net is set to dig just a little too much it is inclined to lift the brutes. Sometimes it takes two boats working in a combined operation to get them out of the water.

I don't suppose anyone ever thought of giving the bags 'a wee wash' with the deck hose on calm days ...

It was during the 1972 queenie season that a most flagrant act of opposition against the Campbeltown fleet was committed. A good bed was located in Lamlash Loch and a substantial number of boats pursued the fishing successfully until one vessel came fast on what was no ordinary obstruction. After much effort which went on for hours, the mouth of the net slowly broke surface with a strange shape wedged tightly in its cavernous jaws. Crewmen thought they were seeing things as the body of an Austin 1100 motor car emerged. The men eventually managed to strap the net and car alongside and made slowly for the shore where it was cut free in shallow water.

That incident marked the beginning of a saga which was to last for weeks as more and more boats dragged up cars of every description.

It was claimed that a certain sea angling club, resentful of the fact that professional fishermen were making a living in the loch, chartered a boat to dump old vehicles indiscriminately throughout the area. Factual claims by the skippers that the trawls were not designed to catch fish, borne out by low fish landings, fell on stony ground.

The cost of the escapade in terms of lost time and fishing gear ran to thousands of pounds. Nobody is quite certain just how many vehicles were on the sea bed, but the figure of 15 was mentioned. Any car which broke free of the gear was pinpointed with deadly accuracy by Decca Navigator and skippers worked closely together, enabling boats to avoid the rusting menaces.

It must be said, though, that the incident, carried out in the name of 'sport' left a bitter taste in the mouth.

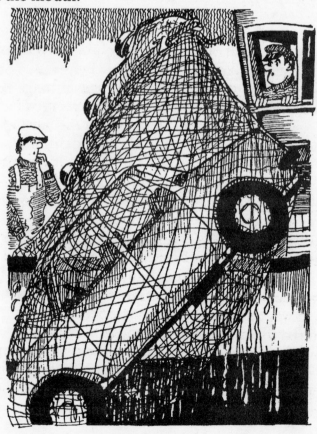

The Podlies

I was still aboard with Andy on the **Girl Margaret** when I had my first taste of midwater pair-trawling and in fact it turned out to be something of a bonanza. This particular fishery involved large saithe, or podlies, as the species is usually called. We partnered Dunure, Ayrshire skipper, 'Noddy' Gibson in the **Mari-Dor** (BA 217).

This operation was inaugurated in Kilbrannan Sound during 1972 by the effervescent skipper Howard McCrindle, of Maidens, Ayrshire in the **Silver Lining** (BA 158), his neighbour boat being the **Elizmor** (BA 163), skippered by Gordon Aitken. Nobody quite realised how heavy the shoals were or the market potential until Howard and Gordon began making some impressive landings. Until this time it was thought that big horse power was required to tow midwater gear but the Ayrshire men proved this theory wrong as their vessels were driven by engines of little more than 100 h.p. Using a scaled-down net they also proved that the podlies were fairly easy to catch.

More and more vessels joined in until, at its peak, I counted 47 pairs of boats on the **Girl Margaret's** radar screen one night. Every Clyde port was represented, along with a contingent from Portavogie, Northern Ireland. The best haul I remember was one 400 boxes for a tow of three hours. Our personal best was 240 boxes for two and a half hours. Gutting was a wearisome task as we had to bend down and pick each individual fish off the deck and many hours were spent in this way. It was all worthwhile, though, when the last box was loaded on to the lorry for transportation to major fish processing concerns in England.

A special morning auction had to be established in Campbeltown to cope with the massive landings, which lasted through November and December of that year. I often wish that someone had taken a photograph of all these boats lying on the still winter waters of Campbeltown loch surrounded by countless thousands of wheeling gulls. It would have presented some picture.

It was at this time that I suffered a rather acute embarrassment in the local Royal Hotel. John Graydon, a newspaperman with the then Glasgow *Evening Citizen* was in town covering an important court hearing and, as an old friend, had inquired as to my whereabouts. News reached me at the harbour via a fish buyer that John wished to see me if possible. As we were not due to sail for a few hours I jumped at the chance of renewing our

acquaintance and drove home where I performed a
meticulous toilet. Washed, shaved and groomed but
still wearing my fishing gear I strode confidently
into the hotel's lounge bar where I immediately
spied a covey of the Glasgow press gang. A few
vigorous handshakes later I was comfortably seated
in the company talking over old times. However, I
was aware that I was drawing curious glances from
the assembled newsmen and eventually John asked
if I always took my work home with me. Puzzled, I
asked him what he meant and he let me know
quietly that there was a decidedly noxious fishy
smell emanating from my person, a fact of which I
was blissfully unaware. A visit to the gents revealed
the source of the offensive odour and I found that a
podlie liver had found its way down my back,
probably during frenzied gutting operations and
was wedged between my heavy shirt and jumper.
Muttering confused apologies I took my leave and
sped homewards once more for a change of
clothing. I don't think I've seen John Graydon
since.

When the podlie fishing showed signs of
tailing off, Andy and Noddy decided to try their
hand at the winter sprat fishing in the lochs on the
west side of Mull, still using the pair-trawl method.

The nets were re-rigged accordingly, with the
standard size fishtail netting being replaced with
the finely-meshed sprat bag. Indeed, the meshes of
this bag are so fine that it can be likened to a pair of

women's fishnet tights. It is impossible to mend a sprat bag in the normal manner and, if damage is done, the edges of the split are gathered together and laced tightly with twine.

I thought we were in for another bonanza when we netted 140 crans (21 tons) in our first haul at Loch Scridain on a Monday afternoon. But that night a storm force ten north-westerly sprang up and the boats had to run for anchor shelter at the head of the loch. It was during that wild night that I learned a very important lesson – the result of an incident which still gives me the 'willies' when I think about it.

Both boats dropped anchor as close in to the weather shore as possible and tied alongside each other. Conditions were so fierce, with the wind screaming down from the high lochside hills, it was decided to set anchor watches in case of mishap. Both engines were stopped and myself and Ian Caldwell, on the **Mari-Dor** were given first watch while the others slept.

As is quite normal with a shrieking north-westerly gale, the sky was clear and the outline of the looming hills under which we lay was perfectly silhouetted in the moonlight. I noted that the **Girl Margaret's** foremast was dead in the centre of a 'v' shaped nick in the hills and decided to use this as a marker. Ian took a similar bearing and this was checked every few minutes. However, what neither of us realised was that we were slowly dragging anchors. Because of the strain on the anchor cables, the position of the boat's heads did not alter, though they were being pushed gradually away from the shore in the direction of a sinister reef that lay into the south-east. I eventually realised that the boat had begun a rolling motion and before I could work out what was happening Andy was on deck with the rest of the crew. He had felt the motion in the forecastle and knew what was taking place.

The boats separated and the anchors were heaved aboard, but as we prepared to steam away clear of the reef the **Mari-Dor's** engine, which had been giving trouble with fuel problems, spluttered to a stop, and minutes later she was aground.

Without hesitation, Andy turned the **Girl Margaret** towards her and nosed carefully in as far as he dared. It was a one-chance situation as the sea was already beginning to pound the other boat and the crew had donned lifejackets. Henry O'Hara, the strongest man in the **Girl Margaret's** crew, hurled a two and a half inch rope with all his might and expertise and it landed neatly on the **Mari-Dor's** deck, to be made fast quickly by eager hands. She was gently eased off the reef and towed well clear to safety. The whole operation could not have lasted more than 15 minutes, but to me it seemed like an agonising lifetime.

I doubt if many publishers would care to go to press with the words my skipper used to me that night, but they were fully deserved. Through pure inexperience I had neglected to perform the simple act of switching on the radar scanner and this would have prevented the incident happening, as the shoreline would have been seen to fade further from the boat.

Andy and I speak about that night even yet and we both agree that it was probably the most valuable piece of experience regarding anchor procedure that I ever gained, though the consequences could have been disastrous. I have been on many anchor watches since, perhaps not in such horrific conditions, but I always made sure that the electronic eye as well as my own has been beamed on the shore.

As it was, the gale blew all that week and we were stormbound in Bunessan until we finally made it to Oban on the Saturday morning. The sprats, which had been in the boats all week, were sold for fishmeal. It was like discharging concrete as we dug into the solid, stinking mass in the hold.

Andy was ashore attending to business with the fishsalesman when we eventually finished washing down the boat and I went to find him to ask if the boat was to be left in Oban for the weekend, so that proper mooring arrangements could be made. At the office I was told that he was having coffee with the agent in a nearby hotel and I ventured in, the prospect of a long cool drink spurring me on. Andy took one sniff, handed me £5 and told me to go somewhere else!

That, however, was the end of the excursion
to the sprats as both skippers decided that the boats
were too small for the west coast winter conditions
and we retreated through the Crinan Canal for a
further podlie hunt.

I also enjoyed a few weeks' podlie fishing in partnership with Nigel McCrindle in the **Peaceful Waters** in the autumn of 1979.

We fished in Loch Long, the snake-like offshoot of the River Clyde and though we were confined to a small area as the lower loch is largely restricted to MoD activities, fishing was good. We were taking valuable codling, lythe and hake as well as the ubiquitous podlie, landing on alternate days at Largs, from whence the fish went by road to the Ayr market. Despite the fact that gales blew for two weeks we did not lose a single day's fishing in the loch's confined waters.

It was while fishing here that we came across a remarkable character who operated a fleet of drift nets from a small coracle type of open boat. He appeared alongside the **Golden Fleece** as we were towing one day, an elf-like figure with a large beakish nose and sporting a woollen hat which I am sure had seen service as a tea cosy. He was a most amiable chap and we took to him immediately, even when he said he had drift nets set and would we please look out for them. This proved to be no easy task as their presence could only be detected by a series of old liquid detergent bottles dotted along the surface. The crew of the **Golden Fleece** christened him 'Findus' and we became good friends over the next week or two.

While lying in Carrick Castle having a well-earned break, we discovered that Findus was a

Glaswegian 'refugee' who had settled in a caravan on the shores of Loch Goil. The fact that he had no prior knowledge of fishing or boats did not deter him from becoming a full-time fisherman.

Nigel and I had a closer look at his boat and saw immediately that she was leaking badly and that the level of water was almost touching a monstrous uncovered flywheel which was attached to the ancient diesel. We bailed out the boat and since Findus was nowhere to be seen, left word at the village shop that his boat was making water, a message which the storekeeper accepted with nonchalance. We discovered the reason the next morning when, while observing Findus going about his business, a huge water spout shot upwards from his boat. Apparently the leak was permanent and the rotating flywheel served as an excellent bilge pump when the water reached its level. I can still see these sudden flying waterspouts in my mind yet.

As a favour, we took Findus' catch to Largs when going to land and it never consisted of more than a few stones of fish worth the same amount of pounds but he was always delighted with the money he received. It was not surprising, therefore, to find that on snagging his nets one night while towing in darkness, they were seen to be full of more large holes than meshes. As a consolation, we presented him with an eight-stone box of prime cod, which delighted him no end.

Towards the end of the fishery, the **Peaceful**

Water's engine suffered a severe malfunction and we had to escort him to Greenock, the nearest port serviced by marine engineers.

When the waterfront population heard we were in the Victoria Dock, hordes of people arrived down looking for a 'fry'. Campbeltown men are renowned for giving away free fish – within reason – to people on the quayside. But this time the entire catch would have disappeared if we had to accommodate everyone's request, so we had to refuse.

Later, a crew member on one of the old Clyde puffers came aboard and offered us a deal. He explained that his boat was on a supply contract with the US Navy Base in Holy Loch and would give us a box of 'goodies' in return for a box of fish. This was readily agreed and we waited in eager anticipation for his return. With a shout of 'ahoy', a large canvas bag thudded on to the deck and he made off. Talk about being conned – the bag contained the oldest, smelliest collection of sea clothing I have ever seen, ranging from soiled T-shirts to greasy boiler suits. The boat in question was, in fact, on contract to the US Navy, but in the capacity of a floating dustcart.

Bomber was later told in no uncertain terms by an officer of the Greenock Constabulary to remove from his person the jacket of a US Navy Captain, complete with insignia, which he had donned for a stroll through the town.

Heavy Metal

THE late Donald McConnachie, a well-read Carradale fisherman noted for his sagacious observations and comments on the fisherman's lot once described clam fishing thus:

"Everything you touch weighs a hundredweight."

The man was not far wrong and yet it remains my favourite occupation for a variety of reasons, despite being easily the most dangerous of all fishing jobs.

Clam fishing or, more precisely, dredging, is a world apart from trawling in that it is carried out chiefly in shallow water close to land. The nature of the seabed can be firm, sandy, corally, shelly or stony, as compared to the heavy muddy bottom which the prawn frequents. The ground is ploughed by metal dredges, rather than a net.

A clam dredge is a steel, triangular-shaped affair, two feet six inches broad at its base. Protruding downwards from this base is a bar to which eight or ten sharp steel teeth of six inches in

69

length are welded. This bar is known as a sword and is set to dig the clams out of their semi-buried positions. The shells are retained in a chain-mail bag which travels along the bottom attached to the sword. To prevent the clams escaping, the top of the chain bag is covered with heavy duty synthetic netting.

On original clam dredges, which could be anything up to six feet broad, the sword was bolted solidly to the frame. However, thanks to an innovation by skipper John King, of Kirkcudbright, all swords are now spring-loaded, which enables them to 'give' on hard stony ground, greatly reducing the gathering of rocks. Although there are many variations, the basic idea is to work slack springs on stony ground, tightening in stages as the ground becomes cleaner and firmer.

The apex of each dredge is shackled at equal intervals to a towing bar, sometimes constructed of a length of four-inch box steel or similar, and they are linked together by small lengths of chain. The bar, in turn, is fitted with five heavy chain bridles which come together at a central towing point at the end of the trawl warp. This wire is much heavier than the type used at prawn trawling.

The amount of dredges towed is dependent on the vessel's size and horse power. Smaller type boats in the 40 foot category usually work three dredges per side while the 'big boys' can tow seven or eight off each quarter.

The boats have to have protection from this type of gear. Strip steel cladding is fitted to their hulls, the length of which is in accordance with the spread of gear worked.

'Outriggers', which jut some feet clear of the boat, are fitted on the lowest point on each quarter and the towing warps pass through running blocks shackled to their outmost extremity. When the gear is hauled to the point of the outrigger it is thus kept clear of the hull.

At this stage a two foot long solid steel hook, which is shackled to the end of a three inch nylon double purchase block and tackle, is fitted into an equally strong ring at the end of the towing wire. The winch operator then takes three or four turns round the whipping barrel, heaving by hand in a steady manner.

The brakes are slowly, but simultaneously, slackened until the block and tackle has the full weight of the gear, at which point they are let off completely.

The dredges are now under the complete control of the winchman, who steadily heaves them along the boat's hull to the central lifting point, a well stayed 20-foot high steel derrick. The dredges now rise vertically out of the water, sliding up the steel cladding until the teeth slip into a specially fitted steel channel on the gunwhale. As the winchman gradually takes the turns off, crewmen position themselves at the bar and push it down on to the deck.

The dredges which are still hanging over the side but held by the teeth, are emptied in a tipping fashion by way of a lighter hook which 'fishes' a bight of rope attached to the end of the chain bag.

I think this is the most dangerous part of the job. If the dredges are full of stones, which frequently happens, there is a possibility that the tremendous weight of the overhanging gear will take charge, causing the bar to shoot upwards and back over the side. The bar, in fact, has sometimes to be winched down to deck level, the crew being powerless to land it – (more about that later).

The clams are separated from the assorted debris and thrown into the middle of the boat. When the stones and rubbish have been shovelled back into the sea – a strength-sapping test of endurance – the shells are counted by the dozen and put into sacks.

Main buyers are Young's Scottish Seafoods and the clams are transported to the Annan factory every two days, where they are shelled, cleaned and frozen. Most of the clams are exported, mainly to France, where demand is high.

As running repairs are often carried out to the gear, spares of every description are usually kept on deck. Clam men, therefore, have to literally watch every step they take. Many a grazed shin and nipped finger I have suffered through a momentary lack of concentration.

Why, then, is it my favourite form of fishing? The main reason is that, unlike trawling, the boats are seldom out more than one day at the same spot and I enjoy the ever-changing scenery. Like all occupations, a feeling of drudgery sometimes sets in at the fishing and a visit to different shores helps to alleviate this.

I also like the brevity of the hauls which, on average, are of about 45 minutes' duration. This way it is possible to see at a glance how progress is going, rather than the four hour wait at trawling. It also helps to make the working day seem shorter and more exciting.

It would be impossible to work clam gear in the conditions endured by the prawn men and, consequently, operations invariably take place in the lee of the land, which helps to make life more pleasant.

While the Coal Tar make periodic forays to the clams, it is the neighbouring Carradale fleet which has made the job its mainstay. Indeed, Ronnie has made clam fishing his life and has followed nothing else for the past 20 years. From small beginnings he is now the proud owner of a fine modern vessel, **Bonnie Lass 3** (CN 126).

Though Ronnie never strays from the Clyde and Sound of Jura grounds, his consistently high grossings over the years have led to his local title of 'King Clam'.

On the national side of things, the legendary

John McAlister is the undisputed monarch of the fishery. A Gigha man now resident in Oban, John travels far and wide – he's even been to Fair Isle – in the 60-foot **Star of Annan** (OB 50) in search of the shells. Completely devoted to scallop fishing also, his grossings for 10-day trips are nothing short of remarkable.

Notable Campbeltown clam skippers include John McKerral, Norman Hunter, Denis Meenan (now retired) and brother Robert. Dare I say I "wasn't bad at it" myself?

Though stocks are now drastically reduced clams can be found along the entire Scottish west coast and the islands. Robert and Denis made successful trips as far out as the Uists.

Prices have reached an all-time high and processors have paid an unheard of £6 to £7 per dozen for good quality, such is the clam's popularity – and scarcity.

As with other species of shellfish, different areas produce clams of varying quality. The deeper the water, the poorer the meat yield seems to be.

A typical case in point is the comparison of grounds – a mere few miles apart – at Craighouse, Isle of Jura and the area around the mouth of West Loch Tarbert. The Craighouse clams, which lie at the edge of the sand and mud, are infamously small while the West Loch shells are real monsters. I once weighed the meat of a West Loch scallop and it tipped the scales at a staggering half pound, almost a meal in itself.

The heaviest concentrated clam fishery ever seen in the Firth of Clyde was discovered not by one of the 'experts' but by accident.

Prawn fishing was slow and Nigel in the **Peaceful Waters** decided to try his luck for demersal fish, using his usual trawl, in a position some four miles south-south-east of Sanda Island. Barely ten minutes had elapsed before he came fast on the firm bottom and, when the gear was heaved aboard, five dozen large clams were seen to be in the cod end.

Clams are occasionally lifted by trawling gear and, indeed, it is a sign that there is a reasonable bed thereabouts, but to net five dozen in ten minutes was unprecedented.

Nigel kept his secret for a year, until he eventually rigged the boat for dredging and was able to go back to the area. We were clam fishing in the **Golden Fleece** at the time and on hearing that Nigel had made a good landing I asked one of his crew at the weekend where they had been fishing.

"Och, down at Ailsa Craig. but I think we've cleaned up the wee spot," I was told.

In a somewhat sceptical frame of mind, I made for Paddy's Milestone on the Monday morning, a day I remember as being decidedly fresh from the southward with poor visibility. After circumnavigating the rock and finding no trace of Nigel, I decided to call him on the radio and ask him for his position.

Using telephone numbers in a cryptic fashion in place of Decca Navigator co-ordinates he unselfishly reported where he was and, on consulting the chart, I did not entirely believe him. However, we steamed off west and eventually picked up a target on the radar which coincided with his reported position.

I really thought I had been the victim of the practical joke of the century. There we were, miles from anywhere in the middle of a vicious tide and a strong breeze of wind. And to even contemplate shooting the gear in 28 fathoms of water seemed ludicrous.

However, comforted by the fact that Nigel was there also, we tried a haul. To the disgruntled crew's astonishment a short tow yielded 32 dozen huge clams. Unfortunately the wind rose alarmingly and both boats had to run for Campbeltown after a short time, but that was the beginning of the 'Sanna Fishing', as it became known later.

There were two important aspects which had to be watched while fishing there. The first was the weather and tide, a fearful combination when the wind was southerly and the tide was on the ebb. This is a classic case of tide going through wind, but it was made all the worse by the area's exposed position. Secondly, tows had to be short as the coral seabed was covered with sea grass, a pleasantly sweet-smelling form of seaweed. This growth clogged up the netting in the dredges which meant that the grit could not escape. Each dredge was filled to capacity every haul.

As the news gradually leaked out about the big landings, more vessels began to filter on to the scene until the expected armada arrived. A total of 49 boats from ports as far distant as the Isle of Man, Wales and Ireland, and including all Clyde clammers, relentlessly fished the area. which, incidentally, was no more than two square miles, for about a month.

Ronnie was there in the **Bonnie Lass 2** and I remember the day he cautioned Skipper Willie Lennon, of Donaghadee, Co Down, when the latter shot his gear directly in front of him, an event which was bound to happen in the congestion.

Willie, in an attempt to make light of the incident, attempted a touch of the Irish blarney over the radio but Ronnie was not impressed and was further outraged when the inevitable happened, the two boats' gear became foul of one another. The result was that a total of 12 four-foot dredges locked together in such a manner that would have made Houdini think twice emerged at the starboard quarter on the **Bonnie Lass 2.**

Skipper Lennon, also cox of Donaghadee Lifeboat, came alongside to retrieve his gear and Ronnie, who had been keeping up a running commentary on the radio, announced:

"In the name of Scotland, there's a dog in the middle of everything".

It appeared that Willie Lennon, a canine lover of note, never put to sea without his beloved Jack Russell terrier and the dog scuttled about the deck in gay abandon, utterly oblivious to what was going on around him.

Some of my finest fishing acquaintances from ports other than Campbeltown were made at the clams. These include big Jim Prentice and Ian McKay, of Tarbert, who were skipper and mate respectively of the **Jura** (OB 123). Another is John McAlister, already mentioned.

Two Ayrshire men of repute are Norman 'Fizzy' Davidson, skipper-owner of the **Strathdoon** (BA 116) and Jimmy 'Dimbo' Milne, of the **Sea Otter** (BA 6) . Add skippers Davy and Benny Nicolson of Kirkcudbright, and we have a truly mixed bag. As well as being excellent fishers of clams, the afore-mentioned gentlemen were good mates and I tended to keep company with them, both on sea and land. Tobermory, on Mull, was our favourite gathering place and many an entertaining run ashore was enjoyed in the port.

A full-blooded Highland ceilidh was in progress one evening in the village hall and Jim Prentice bet me £1 that I wouldn't dare ask a particularly buxom young lady to partner me in an eightsome reel, a wager immediately accepted and won. It was a well-earned pound, I may add,

because I was 'reeling' myself for half an hour afterwards, such was her enthusiasm for dancing.

The following morning, while towing on a particularly clean piece of ground off Mull's Cailleach Point, it became apparent to us that the springs on our dredges required tightening to a considerable extent as they came up like empty envelopes three tows in succession. It was found that the adjusting nuts were solidly-seized and no amount of effort would shift them. Jim with typical generosity offered to lend us a complete set of new springs and when we went alongside to pick them up he hailed me audibly in the broad Tarbert drawl:

"It would be fine if ye could catch the bulk o' that big yin ye were dancin' with last night."

McKay the mate loved what he called a 'terr' and made it his business to be the instigator of many a practical joke.

The **Jura** was nearing the end of an eight day trip and Jim happened to mention he was in need of a clean set of jeans to travel home in and intended to rinse out a pair. He later discovered that the trousers were missing from his bunk. The mystery was solved only when McKay produced them from a dredge newly hauled from the water with the words:

"What better could you ask for than a pair of stone-washed denims?"

A huge anchor which at one time held fast a sailing schooner has been lying in state at Gigha Pier for some years now. I wonder how many people know the story behind it? I certainly do. While spending one of my frequent weekends on the island, I found out that a team of divers engaged in the underwater demolition of an old wreck in a few fathoms of water just off the pier had picked up 120 dozen big clams. I was assured by the men that it was a completely isolated bed and no other scallops were seen in the vicinity.

However, no amount of reasoning would persuade my then skipper, Colin Oman, that the divers were telling the truth and, sure enough, we shot the gear in the little strait between Gigha and Gigalum Isle a few days later.

After about twenty minutes the boat slowed down and we heaved aboard a tangled mess of metal incorporating dredges, chains and the anchor. It took three hours of hauling, manhandling and abundant use of rich expletives before we managed to land the anchor on the pier. The absence of even a single clam was conveniently forgotten.

How true were Donald McConnachie's words.

I was once completely hoodwinked by a pleasant, good-humoured minesweeper captain during a call at Brodick, Arran.

We were dredging for clams in the **Golden Fleece** close inshore in the Brodick area and, while no records were being broken, fishing was steady.

I met the gentleman in question while enjoying a beer in the village's Douglas Hotel and he seemed genuinely interested in what we were doing. After a lengthy chat on the subject he told me that some of his divers had found a substantial clam bed in Brodick Bay. He offered to give me the exact position and I spent an hour with him and his first officer on the minesweeper's bridge poring over a large scale chart of the area.

Armed to the teeth with bearings, cross-bearings, depths and landmarks I set off early next morning and, full of expectations, towed over the position for an hour and a half. I could hardly look when the six dredges came up when we hauled and I wished that I had not. The entire catch consisted of one rusty camera and a ship's wine bottle – empty of course. Despite the 'white of the eye' look from the crew I tried again… and again until I had to concede that I had been the victim of a practical joke.

I bear no grudge against the man as it is the type of thing I would probably do myself.

By far the most tiring and soul-destroying occupation I have ever had was as a deckhand on an Irish queenie dredger. The Kirkcudbright fleet follow this type of fishing on a year-round basis on grounds ranging from the Solway Firth to the Welsh coast using four-foot dredges in preference to trawls as the ironmongery seems to suit the type of bottom better.

It all started when the **Forards** (B 300), of Portavogie, came to Campbeltown to be fitted out for the job. The 73-foot steel boat, built as a 'sputnik' class trawler for Fleetwood in the sixties, had a new heavy duty winch and lifting derricks installed and was, indeed, ideal for the queenie fishing. Incidentally, she is the best sea boat I have ever sailed on.

I met the skipper, Fergie Hughes, of Ballywalter, Co. Down, on Campbeltown's New Quay and it transpired he was looking for another man to make up a crew of six and I was duly shipped. After calling briefly at Portavogie for stores and fuel we set off with high hopes for the Morecambe Bay area where a good number of Kirkcudbright men were towing.

From the word go it was evident that this was no ordinary fishery. The eight dredges filled to capacity in 40 minutes and the bulk was strewn over a length of 15 feet, piled up flush with the boat's rail. The boat was equipped with two queenie riddles, electrically-operated revolving drums which separated the queenies from unwanted coral, broken shell, small stones and so on. The riddles had to be fed by shovelling the assorted mess into one end, the 'clean' queenies being ejected at the other. It took five of us 35 minutes to clear the deck and basket the queenies before bagging and stowing below. Five minutes later we were faced with the same solid mixture.

No navvy has worked so hard as the crew of the **Forards** did for the next 23 hours. Apart from hastily-devoured sandwiches and half mugs of tea in odd minutes spent in the galley we were on deck shovelling, bagging and stowing the whole time. At the end of it all it was discovered that we had a total of 57 bags below – considerably short of the viable target of 100 we had set.

Fergie, though perhaps not physically exhausted but nevertheless a very tired man, stopped the engine and switched on the two 'not under command' red mast lights. We rolled into our bunks without as much as taking off a single item of clothing and the next six hours were spent in unconscious oblivion. On awakening I discovered muscles I did not even know I had.

A further 24 hours of non-stop toil, made worse by riddles clogging up every now and then, saw us with another 62 bags and we set off for Whitehaven, Cumbria, to land. It was here that one of the crew, Billy Sharp, decided he had fallen victim to an attack of 'influenza' and embarked on the long road and sea journey home to Portavogie. As it was, we soldiered on for a further five days before agreeing that what we were doing could hardly be called fishing, and it was a happy crew that reverted to clamming around the Isle of Man and the Ulster coast.

The Kirkcudbright men are experts at queenie dredging but it comes as no surprise to me that the boats have an exceedingly high turn round of crewmen. Personally speaking there will be banana trees growing on Morecambe Pier before I ever shoot a queenie dredge again.

Neighbours

AS I have mentioned earlier, herring fishing from
Campbeltown – a port which only a generation ago
could boast the finest fleet of ring-netters in the
country – is now carried on by one pair of boats, the
Nova Spero and **Brighter Morn.**

They work the mid-water trawl method to a
high degree of efficiency and are probably the top
herring men in the Firth of Clyde.

Though Campbeltown lost most of its ringers
in the mid-fifties due to a disastrous slump in
herring stocks it was the deadly catching power of
the pair-trawl which finally sentenced ring-netting
to death.

Horse-power is an all-important factor in
herring pair-trawling and the two Campbeltown
boats have identical 450 h.p. Caterpillar engines
installed. They tow a net which has a huge mouth
opening of 90 feet by 90 feet and a length of some
200 yards between them. The pair-trawl can be
used by day or night and can be put right down to
the clean bottom in deep water if necessary.

In the last few years fisheries department scientists have imposed a total allowable catch for each Clyde season. A quota system, vigorously policed by Department of Agriculture and Fisheries for Scotland officials, is in operation throughout the season, the duration of which is about five months.

The herring week begins at midnight on Sunday and ends with Thursday morning's sale, an equal amount being landed daily. Should a pair fail to catch their daily allocation it is permissible to 'double up' the following day.

Herring in the Clyde are located chiefly in Kilbrannan Sound, the Lady Isle Bank, Inchmarnock Water ('east sound') and in Lochs Long, Goil and Striven. The boats prowl systematically over known herring grounds and steam about one mile apart.

Sophisticated electronic detection equipment, some of which can record a single fish, is deployed. The introduction some ten years ago of the colour video echo sounder has been a great boon to the herring skipper. Different species of fish show on the television screen and it is now possible to tell if the boat is on top of herring by the deep red picture and certain other features.

The fishlupe is a form of sonar which works in conjunction with the traditional paper recording sounder. The screen is divided by a continually flashing thin line. When a heavy shoal shows up on the sounder, the fishlupe line spreads out

Christmas tree fashion and the type of fish can be identified by the shape of the 'branches'.

Perhaps the most important addition to the herring man's wheelhouse aids recently has been the net sounder.

This clever invention has three parts – a transducer mounted on the headline of the net, a paravane which 'swims' a few feet below the boat and a recording unit in the wheelhouse. The battery-powered transducer or 'bomb' as it is called, beams a signal from the net to an eye on the paravane. An electric cable carries the 'picture' up into the bridge where it shows on the recorder.

As well as clearly identifying the top and bottom ropes of the net, the unit has all the characteristics of a traditional sounder in that the seabed and shoals of fish can be seen also. The herring are actually recorded entering the mouth of the trawl and it is simple to gauge how much is in the net. What would the Coal Tar of old think of it all?

Each vessel carries a net which is completely prepared to shoot at a minute's notice. The mid-water trawl is made up of several sections, or 'panels', and the mesh size at its mouth can be anything up to an almost unbelievable 15 feet. The bigger the mesh, the less resistance and the net is thus easier to tow. The panels decrease in size gradually down to the one-inch herring bag.

The basic theory is that the fish are confused

by the turbulence created by the net's mouth travelling through the water and, unable to see the small mesh at the end of the bag, swim in that direction for what appears to be an escape route.

When the net is shot the neighbour boat comes alongside to pick up one end of the trawl. Attached to the top and bottom of the net are combination wire/rope bridles, or 'sweeps' of eight and twelve fathom lengths respectively. These are clipped on to the neighbour's warps and the boats separate to a distance checked by radar – determined by the length of wire to be used which depends on the depth of the shoal. The net is helped on its downward path by 600lb weights shackled to the end of each bottom sweep.

When hauling, the boats come together and strap alongside each other with 25 fathoms of wire to come. When this has been winched up the end is passed back aboard the shooting vessel and the net ends are put into the power block sheave to be pulled in by eager hands. This is when the stinging jelly fish vent their spleen on the herring men. Although they are trapped in the meshes on leaving the water they are squeezed out by the revolving power block and fall towards deck, often coming into contact with susceptible faces en route.

It is unusual to net a complete quota of marketable herring in one tow and many hours are spent selecting the large from the mixed deck cargo. Both boats take an equal amount from the net and the resultant picked herring are boxed and iced below decks.

Modern day buyers insist that the fish should be the maximum size and this means that thousands of perfectly good herring are often discarded in the selection process. Conservatively speaking I would say that the herring dumped in the course of a week's herring fishing in the Firth of Clyde would feed an entire Ethiopian village for three months.

Although the **Nova Spero** and **Brighter Morn** mainly use the herring landing port of Tarbert, Loch Fyne, the first few weeks of the season are spent in Ayrshire waters, discharging at Ayr. It was here when working on the **Brighter Morn** that I came across two notable worthies known to me only as Sam and Mugsie. These middle-aged entrepreneurs appointed themselves ship's runners, one to each boat. In return for a basket of herring daily, the intrepid pair attended to the supply of rolls and newspapers. Rain, hail or shine they were there on Ayr Harbour without fail.

Mugsie was our man and joined us for breakfast, over which he would audibly condemn Sam for serious misdeeds allegedly committed the night before in some Burns country howf. Meanwhile, in the **Alliance's** forecastle, a similar performance would take place, with Mugsie being the offender. It was comical, therefore, to see the pair of them later ride off like bosom buddies on their bicycles with freshly filleted herring to sell round the housing estates.

Sam arrived without wheels one morning and sheepishly informed us that he couldn't remember which pub he had left his bike outside the previous night. However, he was fully equipped with a suitable conveyance inside one hour and I don't know yet where it came from.

Another morning he spied three little cormorants ('dookers') which had unfortunately become entangled in our nets and had drowned. He was seen shortly afterwards disappearing in the direction of a waterfront Chinese restaurant to offer his 'ducks' for sale.

We had only to casually mention the need for some small article or other within their earshot and sure enough the item would be spirited aboard a little later with no questions asked.

I have a super sleeping bag for use on board ship, the result of a remark I made about feeling cold in my bunk one night. Mugsie appeared the following morning with the heavily-padded bag still in its polythene wrapper.

With a nod and a wink he said:

"Yer wee tootsies will be warm in this thing Fred."

All offers of payment were refused and relentless inquiries as to its origin drew a complete blank. Sometimes when I curl up in its cosy confines I feel a pang of guilty conscience but this soon disappears as the waves of slumber envelop me.

Basking sharks are one of the deadliest enemies of herring fishermen When a shark enters a herring trawl the result is invariably a bad tearing in the bag which takes hours of painstaking mending since the mesh is so small. Even if the beast manages to escape it is easy to tell shark damage by the thick deposits of its bodily slime left on the netting.

We caught a huge specimen in Kilbrannan Sound during one poor night in 1976. The **Alliance** was at that time partnering the **Silver Searcher** (CN 245), skippered by the late Davy Paterson. When it became obvious we had a shark in the net, skipper Paterson tried to get alongside to put his crew aboard to assist but the heavy seas prevented this, especially since his boat was built of steel and damage would probably have been done.

The shark, which was 30 feet long if it was an inch, wedged itself in the codend and no amount heaving and winching would budge it. We were left with no alternative but to cut the net to free it and the shark made off wearing a 'coat' of expensive nylon netting. Naturally, the herring we had caught were lost and it was sickening to watch them spew out of the open net in all directions.

Why are some sea anglers so embittered towards full-time fishermen? I asked myself that question one evening in Loch Goil.

Alliance and **Aquila** were having a look in the Loch for herring and we cruised to its head. Like so many sea water lochs, the shores are sheer and it is possible to take a sizeable boat really close to the land. We turned at the head of the loch and, taking a side each, meandered back down some 30 yards from the beach. All of a sudden, we were the target of a hail of stones, some of which were hits, and a torrent of abuse from a group of anglers on the shore.

How I wish that these men would realise that in such situations an easily-torn mid-water net would not be allowed to touch the rough bottom and would be nowhere near their precious undersized saithe which they so much delight in catching.

I may add that before departing the area we got rid of unwanted shackles and other assorted chandelry in a rather unorthodox fashion – by firing the bits and pieces shorewards.

Anyone who has ever had a gun trained on a spot roughly between the eyes will appreciate how I felt one balmy evening in September 1985. **Alliance** and **Aquila** were making for Loch Striven via the Kyles of Bute following reports of herring marks being seen there. As we neared the mouth of the loch, a 75-foot Admiralty type vessel appeared on the scene and closed with **Aquila.** Using a loud hailer, the navy skipper ordered us to stop as he slid alongside. Despite the fact that the boats were

touching each other, he continued to address us
through his megaphone and we remarked quietly

to each other how comical he looked. That was until two ratings raised automatic rifles and pointed them directly at crewman John Newlands and myself. The utter fear and astonishment we felt defies description. He kept repeating:

"Identify yourselves as red forces".

This left us completely bewildered until somebody on board remembered that a big scale NATO exercise was in progress on the Scottish west coast at the time and we were in the vicinity of an Admiralty oil installation, albeit on passage. On his command "Keep clear of the oil jetty" we steamed speedily off. The parting shot from an **Aquila** crewman who shall remain nameless was an instruction to the navyman to commit an act upon himself which is biologically impossible.

We later discovered that the 'commander' in question was in the naval reserve and revelled in playing war games. Fair enough, but I certainly felt no easier when I was assured that the guns were well and truly loaded.

At the close of the herring season, the **Nova Spero** and **Brighter Morn** turn to sprat fishing which, with luck, can last until Christmas. The same nets are used, but the herring bag is replaced with the tiny-meshed sprat tail.

The sprats generally frequent lower Loch Fyne, the Ardlamont area of Inchmarnock Water and the upper reaches of Kilbrannan Sound, though they have periodically been caught in other areas.

Sprats are similar in appearance to herring, though very much smaller, growing to a maximum of six inches. Frosty weather tends to cause them to shoal thickly and such conditions are eagerly awaited by sprat men.

The large and juicy Clyde sprats are in keen demand and are usually bought by a Fraserburgh concern which has a big canning plant in the town.

Because of the density of the shoals it would be impracticable to box the sprats on deck and they are kept in bulk in the specially prepared fish room. They are let into the hold through manholes on deck, to which wooden chutes are clamped. One man is stationed below to keep the vessel in trim while the sprats are taken aboard. To ensure that the boat stays on an even keel, wing compartments on either side are filled alternately and the hold man has to keep the fish running by using a special shovel. Bilge pumps are in constant use throught the operation to cope with the massive volume of water which comes aboard.

I was hold man aboard the **Aquila** and I shall never forget one glorious morning at Claonaig, in Kilbrannan Sound when we filled the boat to capacity in one haul. After shovelling the sprats into her I had to descend again and empty her at Tarbert. Not suprisingly I had three complete changes of clothing in 16 hours, due to being drenched in sweat. We discharged 27 tons, the

Alliance 19, to give a total landing of 46 tons. This represents something in the order of two and a quarter million sprats.

As soon as the sprats are unloaded, the hold must be meticulously washed and scrubbed with strong detergent as the fish in a compressed state give off a noxious gas. If allowed to build up, this gas will turn a brass porthole black in a matter of two days. It is obviously important to empty the boat as quickly as possible.

There was a heavy sprat fishing several years ago in the North Sea and a large fleet was landing into North Shields, Tyne and Wear. Such was the congestion at the port that there were long delays as vessels waited their turn to discharge. One boat of more than 70 feet was loaded to the hatches and the gas built up to such an extent that it actually exploded and lifted the steel deck completely off the cross beams.

In terms of bulk, the biggest haul we ever had on the **Brighter Morn** was taken in lower Loch Fyne in 1988. Conservative estimates put the figure at 80 tons but unfortunately there was a preponderance of immature herring through the catch. By law, no more than ten per cent of small herring is allowed to be landed with sprats and we were left with no alternative but to let them go. The net by this time had formed a huge 'S' shaped sausage on the surface and it took twenty minutes before we towed the last fish out of it.

The winter of 1986 saw the sprats shoaling, amazingly, within the confines of Campbeltown Loch, and the **Alliance** and **Aquila** took full advantage of this. Townspeople watched in amazement as the boats shot the gear away only feet from the burgh's Old Quay.

A huge haul was taken by Robert one morning and despite the efforts of both crews at the **Alliance's** power block the full net just would not surface. An attempt was made to raise the net by

Alliance (CN 187)

towing at full speed but this resulted in the £3,000 sprat bag bursting free and sinking to the bottom. Efforts to retrieve the gear with hooks failed and a diver could not even locate the bag in the loch's murky depths.

It says much for the comradeship of Campbeltown fishermen in that a friend of skipper Finn's, lobsterman Archie Graham of Peninver, towed a line over the area each day on returning from his creels. His efforts were eventually rewarded when he successfully snagged the gear some weeks later and it was recovered intact.

Incidentally, the bag was lost a mere 200 yards from the front door of Robert's lochside villa.

Sometimes a heavy concentration of tiny red shrimps of no commercial value are taken along with the sprats and this causes problems getting the cargo below. The shrimp prevents the sprats from running freely in a silvery avalanche and it has been known for boats to let substantial catches go, being unable to do anything with the mixture.

On the **Alliance** and **Aquila** we had a length of the wider meshed herring bag sewn in between the end of the net and the sprat tail. If we had the bad luck to be affected by the shrimp nuisance, it was a simple matter of winching the catch back to the herring bag section. All hands leaned over the side and gave the net a 'good shaking', thus allowing the shrimps to escape through the slightly larger mesh, but retaining the sprats.

One fine November afternoon both crews were busily engaged on board the **Aquila** doing just that and Robert, alone on the **Alliance** kept her on station a few yards from us. He was taking a keen interest in the proceedings when he suddenly let out a roar of laughter – once more at my expense.

The previous weekend in one of the Campbeltown hostelries I happened to mention to a young lady in the company that I greatly admired the sweater she was wearing. She said it was actually a little on the large side for her and she asked me if I would like to have it to wear at sea, an offer graciously accepted and sealed with a gin and tonic. However, it could not have been all that oversized for her because, as Trapper announced with glee to all and sundry, when I leaned over the side to shake the net, two large bumps were clearly visible in the chest region. I'm willing to bet that I am the only fisherman ever to haul a net attired in a 36D cup jumper.

An offshoot of mid-water trawling by two boats is pelagic trawling. The same net is used but is towed by one vessel only, being held open by special mid-water trawl doors

Expensive hake, which swim mainly off the bottom, and cod are sought at this method, which takes place in the deep water (80-100 fathoms) in the Firth of Clyde and was pioneered once again by Howard McCrindle. Because of the scarcity of the species, tows can last anything up to 20 hours.

Tommy Finn, when not pair trawling with Robert, has made this method his mainstay and has, indeed, become expert at the job, having made many notable landings. I was pelagic fishing with Tommy on the **Aquila** when we were dealt a really cruel blow. The hauling process was about to commence when the boat came to an abrupt halt. On heaving back on the gear, it was obvious we had a hold of something heavy and only gentle coaxing of the bar-tight warps got the doors up.

Eventually, the ends of the net were put in the power block but after only a few feet of hauling the hydraulics blew off, rendering the block useless. Radio conversations with other skippers established that we had gripped one of the submarine listening devices which abound in the area, the Decca co-ordinates of which we did not have.

I'll never forget the look on Tommy's face as he handed me a knife and told me to cut away the £6000 net.

Unmentionables

CAMPBELTOWN fishermen through the ages have always been a highly superstitious breed of men although cynics find it easy to treat their beliefs with contempt. But as one brought up in a fishing household I learned early to respect the various 'rules', the breaking of which earned a polite but firm parental rebuke.

Obviously as the years went by I built up a powerful aversion to the use of certain words and actions. On reflection, I must have seemed to be slightly lacking in grey matter to my schoolfriends and teenage mates but that is the way it was.

I doubt if anyone in living memory can explain the origins of the different superstitions and I hope the reader will understand that it is an inborn experience among fisherfolk. We do not subscribe to paganism and I would like to think myself as good a Christian as the next man but on the whole it is a subject which is treated with cautionary seriousness as luck has always played a part in fishing.

I positively cringe as I write words such as rat (long-tailed fellow); rabbit (bunny); pig (doorkie); salmon (buhlly). They are utterly unmentionable.

It is an unpardonable offence to board a Campbeltown fishing boat carrying a familiar brand of matches which features a swan on the box. One must never stick a knife into a boat's mast as this is regarded as being the vessel's heart. And to use a white handled knife is unthinkable. If a fisherman encounters a red-headed woman on his way to the boat he should return home. The same, strangely, applies to a man of the cloth. If a personal item needed for fishing is inadvertently left at home he must sail without it.

Items of clothing do not escape either. There are 'lucky' hats and 'unlucky' hats and a bonnet burned while being dried at the fire should be committed to the deep. Apart from being downright bad manners, all headgear has to be removed before eating at a boat's table. A jumper put on back to front by accident is considered lucky, but it is a bad omen to do this on purpose. Old shoes and boots recovered from the sea in fishing gear are usually retained and placed on top of the wheelhouse roof.

Seagulls, however annoying their ear-piercing screams may be, must not be harmed as an age-old Campbeltown belief maintains that old fishermen return in the after life as herring gulls.

Another sure way of tempting Providence

would be to borrow salt from another boat and to borrow anything on a Monday would undoubtedly ruin the week's fishing. The burning of twine or food is another cardinal sin.

The hauling aboard of a new or repaired net while in harbour has to be carried out while the tide is on the flood and when leaving port the boat should never turn against the sun's path.

The afore-mentioned stipulations must seem ridiculous to the shoresman but would incur the wrath of a Campbeltown skipper if performed on his boat.

An incident during my *Courier* days almost had me stumped. An unfortunate native of the Isle of Islay found himself in front of Sheriff Donald McDiarmid in Campbeltown Sheriff Court to answer poaching charges. As the case unfolded it became obvious to me that the story was worthy of a wider audience and I prepared a version for the Scottish national dailies and the BBC. Needless to say the species was a buhlly and it was mentioned five times in the article.

My editor at that time was Gordon Lang, a highly intelligent man who possessed a sharp wit and a sparkling sense of humour. He was fully conversant with what he called the "nonsensical beliefs of hairy-arsed fishermen" and much to his amusement used his authoritative powers to insist that I telephone this story across.

What a dilemma... I faced having to say the

dreaded word a total of 30 times. Gordon sat back in eager anticipation no more than three feet from me as I ordered the calls. However, during the first one, I was seized with sudden inspiration and when the fateful reference came up I used the nautical phonetic alphabet to spell it out – Sierra, Alpha, Lima, Mike, Oscar, November. All went well until a gruff-voiced male copytaker on the old *Scottish Daily Mail* informed me in the unmistakable Glasgow accent:

"See you Jimmy, yer aff yer heed".

I may add that if an unsuspecting buhlly should accidentally find its way into our nets it is treated with the reverence it deserves, though no mention is made of its name.

One custom which died out long ago, I am glad to record, was "throwing the bunnet". Apparently if a herring fisherman returned to his spouse after a luckless night he had to toss his hat into the bedroom. If it flew back out without a word spoken the weary soul had to make his bed elsewhere, sometimes in his bunk on the boat. I can only assume that these grand old fishermen operated with a degree of competence as many fishing families of that time could have fielded an entire football team without outside aid.

Friday the 13th, or Black Friday, which so many people ashore regard as being a day of ill-luck, holds no special significance to fishermen. I have been fishing many times on that date and

don't remember anything untoward taking place.

A chance encounter with people regarded as being 'lucky' is always welcomed by fishermen.

In my case I always relish an unexpected meeting with my Aunt Lizzie, a sprightly 83-year-old who is out and about every day. A rub on the arm and wish of "good hunting" never fails to produce results. Aunt Lizzie has lost count of the number of prizes she has won in raffles and other games of chance.

Another of my favourites is Mrs Nancy Girvan, former barmaid in Campbeltown's Cabin Lounge. Definitely another 'lucky lady.'

Other unlucky deeds are cutting toe or fingernails on a Sunday, crossing cutlery after a meal and leaving shoes on a table top.

Can a firm and genuine belief in superstition explain spiritualistic phenomena? I was convinced I was psychic following a strange incident in the early seventies.

Preparing to go to sea from Campbeltown on a Sunday evening, Ronnie and I met an ex-deep sea trawler skipper who had given up the howling Barents Sea gales for the comparatively safer life of inshore fishing. His name was David Atkinson, a Fleetwood man, and he was in port with his fine new 70-foot boat **Maritan** (FD 1). A courteous chap, he invited us aboard to share a pot of tea and look around the vessel, a chance we jumped at. After an hour or so of marvelling at the modern equipment we retired to the **Bonnie Lass** and set sail.

Some three weeks later I joined Ronnie in Carradale in readiness for a further week's toil. Though I did not dream of or even think about it the previous night I suddenly asked Ronnie if he had read about the **Maritan's** mishap in *Fishing News*, knowing he was an avid reader of the publication. When he replied in the somewhat bewildered negative I told him that the boat had run aground on the treacherous Torran Rocks near the Isle of Mull, and quoted the page and column number in which the article appeared. He duly consulted the paper and on finding no mention of the story decided I was "havering".

A few days later the **Maritan** went ashore on the Torran Rocks and the following issue of *Fishing News* carried a report of the matter placed in exactly the position I had mentioned. She was, fortunately, successfully refloated.

In the intervening years I have had no further such uncanny experiences apart from the usual "I've been here before" feeling, which many people encounter.

Mishaps

A GREAT many hours are spent by the Coal Tar close inshore, whether it be fishing, on passage or negotiating the many small tricky west coast harbours. There can't be many local fishermen, therefore, who have not been involved in a grounding at some time or other.

The sudden realisation that a boat which has been buoyant and alive has become as immobile as a stranded whale is one of sickening certainty and many fine vessels have been totally wrecked on rocks over the years. It has been my misfortune to have been involved in a few hair-raising escapades which have shaken me considerably.

I was only a few months at the fishing, on the **Brighter Hope,** when I had a frightening experience. And it happened in port. We were fishing for queen scallops on the east side of Arran, none too successfully that particular day, and it was decided to put into Lamlash for the night rather than make the steam to Ardrossan to land the small catch. It was a lovely evening, with just a whisper of easterly wind. The 47 foot boat was moored along the face of Lamlash's little stone pier and as it is a tidal harbour she eventually dried out on the bank at the end of the jetty.

I decided to go ashore and seek out an Arran friend, Alan Little, whom I had not seen for a year or two. I found him and we spent a few hours yarning at his house before I returned to the boat. I noticed on my way back to the pier that the tide was on the flood and there was a little more weight in the wind. It had also changed direction slightly to the north-east. All hands duly turned in and we were soon sound asleep.

As we slept, however, the wind rose to gale force and we were wakened by the boat bumping on the bottom. The waves generated by the wind were lifting the boat off the ground and receding to leave the hull with no water to float in. As the motion grew, running directly through the channel between the Holy Isle and Arran, it became apparent that the **Brighter Hope** was in real danger and the mooring ropes snapped like carrots. There was still insufficient water to float her but she was being thrown mercilessly against the pier and on to the bottom

I managed somehow to clamber up on to the pier with more mooring lines, the intention being to strap them tightly to the wall but they broke hopelessly within seconds of being made fast. As a last resort I was passed up the trawl wire from the winch which I shackled round a bollard.

Ronnie, meantime, had the engine running and the boat in gear astern. As she lifted on a particularly big wave, the **Brighter Hope** suddenly slid off into deeper water. The winch brakes were let off and the wire was allowed to run completely off the drum, leaving me alone on Lamlash Quay at one o'clock in the morning. To attempt to come back in for me would have been suicidal and they stood off.

There was nothing else for it but to pay another visit to my friend and it was a bleary-eyed Alan who answered the door to an oilskinned apparition standing on his doorstep in the wee small hours of the morning.

The next thing I remember is being gently shaken awake by a burly red-headed police sergeant at 8 a.m. He told me the boat was in Brodick, a few miles north, and he was to take me there. The morning was perfect, with blue skies and a flat calm sea. In the space of a few hours the gale had blown itself out. As the police car wound down the steep hill into Brodick the **Brighter Hope** came into view. She looked like a wounded animal which had managed to escape the trapper's snare, with broken and splintered wood very much in evidence. She also had a slight list to starboard.

We limped to McIntyre's Boatyard at Port Bannatyne, near Rothesay, where the boat was slipped. It was three long weeks before the damage was repaired and we were able to resume fishing.

Nine years, thankfully, elapsed before I was to go through another catastrophe, this time in the **Golden Fleece.** Around Easter 1980, we were fishing for clams at the mouth of Loch Sween in company with several other boats. Everyone decided to land at Tayvallich, a picturesque little village at the head of the loch. This was one of the few west coast harbours I had never been in but I knew the entrance was a narrow gap between two jagged reefs and that caution would have to be exercised. As it was going to be pitch black on arrival I decided to hang back and follow the boats through the passage.

I had our bow dead in line with the nearest vessel's stern light on approaching the reefs but unknown to me the skipper made a slight alteration to starboard to avoid a rock which lies between the entrance and the pier. We were, therefore, a shade too far to port and seconds later, with a stomach-churning crunch, the boat clipped the edge of the reef.

She seemed to climb up the rock before being thrown heavily to starboard in the opposite direction with a violent shuddering of masts and superstructure. Although we were off the rock it was a race against time to reach the quay as water was seen to be pouring into the forward accommodation compartment. The remainder of the fleet cast off from the pier to let us get alongside and made fast. The boat was by this time well down by the head and extremely difficult to handle but we got to the jetty and broke out heavy nylon ropes to hold her.

The fire brigade at Lochgilphead, some 14 miles distant, was alerted but much frantic hand pumping had to be carried out before its arrival on the scene. It says much for the comradeship of fishermen in that men from other boats arrived aboard to take a turn operating the pump spear, which is an exhausting business.

Using a powerful portable pump the firemen all but emptied the compartment of seven thousand gallons of seawater in about 15 minutes but we were faced with a sleepless night manning the pump to keep the water level down.

The problem of patching the damage temporarily to allow us to make the long passage to Campbeltown, the nearest suitable slipway, was solved conveniently when three kind gentlemen called on us at first light. They were amateur clam divers – so often the enemy of clam boat skippers – and they gallantly offered their assistance. That was the first time I was ever actually *glad* to see a clam diver.

The trio, headed by one Ian Nicholson, of Milngavie, did a marvellous makeshift repair job using articles such as canvas tarpaulin, pieces of fish boxes and underwater sealant. The leak was reduced to a dribble and we set off for the Mull of

Kintyre though we did have a motorised pump
aboard just in case.

The passage was made without incident but
when the boat slowly rose out of the water at
Campbeltown Shipyard slip we realised how lucky
we had been. Two 12-foot lengths of oak planking
had been badly cracked and there was a hole about
the size of a saucer. I'm sure if the divers had told
us the extent of the damage the voyage would have
been made with more than a little foreboding.

Eight years ago I was at the prawns with Andy
on the **Girl May**. During February of that year we
were working grounds in the Sound of Jura and the
boat was moored at West Loch Tarbert at
weekends.

I was sitting at home watching television one
Sunday evening when a message arrived to the
effect that we would be driving to the West Loch at
midnight, rather than the early hours of the
morning. Andy's friend, the Peterhead skipper
Stuart Finlay of the **Star of Promise** (PD 70), had
been in touch with him to say that his boat was
ashore at Lagg Bay, on Jura, and he requested a
tow off.

High tide the following morning was just
before daybreak and this necessitated the early
start. We arrived in the area in plenty of time and
lay off at a safe distance waiting for the tide to reach
its peak. At the appropriate time we moved slowly
bow-in towards the **Star of Promise**. Our powerful

searchlight's stabbing beam illuminated the scene perfectly and a rope was passed to us quickly and efficiently. With both engines going full astern and the heavy towing line straining to its limit the **Star of Promise** suddenly lurched clear and was once more afloat. All that remained to be done was to let go the towrope and steam away clear but the incredible forces of nature had other plans for us.

The tide by this time had turned and before Andy could swing the **Girl May** to seaward it began running out with such force that the boat was swept sideways towards the south side of the bay. He managed to straighten the boat up just as she came into contact with terra firma and he attempted to 'drive' her off to sea, the only logical manoeuvre he could make.

Unknown to us the reef at this point ran outwards and northwards in an 'L' shape and we were slowly but surely going further on. When it became clear that we were not going to make it Andy summoned the assistance of lobster-man Bill Campbell, of Jura, who had been standing by all the time. Andy gave the order to abandon ship and we were barely aboard the small lobster boat when the **Girl May** heeled over at a 40° angle.

Never before and never since have I seen a tide leave a shore with such ferocity. We were transferred to the **Star of Promise** which by that time was lying safely at anchor in an ample depth of water. Shortly after daylight, Andrew Harrison Jnr.

noticed that the searchlight was still on and, along with crewman Robert McGeachy, bravely volunteered to go out in a dinghy to switch it off in case the batteries drained. It was no easy task rowing the lightweight punt back against the tide.

We spent the day aboard the **Star of Promise** and attempted a tow with the evening tide – to no avail. There was nothing further we could do until the morning and the night was spent at Craighouse Pier, a few miles south of Lagg.

The fact that it was February, a month with a notorious reputation for sudden gales, caused a continuous nagging doubt that conditions might worsen, leaving the boat, which was exposed to wind directions from northerly right down to south-south east, in real danger.

The morning attempt again proved abortive and the situation began to look bleak. The **Alliance** and **Aquila,** both prawn trawling in the Gigha waters since the herring season was closed, offered to come to our aid in a combined effort using their total of 700 h.p.

It was decided, however, to have one further attempt and, at the precise minute of high water that night, the **Star of Promise** jerked us off.

It was an incident I shall always remember as being caused not by human error, but by the viciousness of the ebb tide at Lagg Bay, a place never to be underestimated.

Recollection of the events of St Andrews

Night, 1989 will remain with me for the remainder of my allotted span.

I was once again aboard with Andy, this time on the £200,000 **Strathisla** (CN 240). Until that night we had been fishing extremely well on the grounds surrounding Skerryvore Lighthouse, 10 miles south-south west of Tiree. Skilful use of sonar by Andy had opened up hitherto unfished grounds and we were taking prime fish such as turbot, Dover sole, brill as well as haddock, huge plaice and skate. Based in Oban, we were on the second night out of our third trip to Skerryvore when catastrophe struck.

At 8 p.m. all hands were aft standing by the hydraulic net drum a – large steel spool on to which the net was wound. The net ends had just been clipped on to the drum when Andy roared aft from the bridge: "We are on fire."

Flames were seen shooting from the access hatch and ventilation shafts of the engine room, which was situated forward on the 66-foot vessel. The flames died out as quickly as they had appeared, but thick choking smoke poured from the airways. We immediatley battened down the hatch and stuffed anything available into the ventilators to cut off the air supply.

Meanwhile Andy had managed to send out a Mayday call which was intercepted by Oban Coastguard. Seconds later the boat was plunged into darkness when the electrics failed, obviously burnt out at the power source in the engine room.

Fortunately Andy is a radio buff and he had with him a hand-held VHF unit on which he was able to contact the Coastguard, who informed him that the German cargo ship **Loke** was approximately one hour from us and was making all speed.

In the interim we had launched the inflatable liferaft and donned life-jackets. Tribute must be paid to the Captain of the **Loke** for his skill in manoeuvring the large vessel alongside in the heavy Atlantic swell. By the time we had clambered aboard the coaster, the pitch on the **Strathisla's** deck had begun to melt with the heat.

The **Strathisla** was strapped up alongside the ship and crewmen played powerful hoses over the smouldering fire area in an attempt to keep the heat down. Though thick smoke still escaped there was no sign of flame and we thought there was a good chance of saving the boat.

Barra lifeboat had reached the scene and a SAR helicopter scrambled from Stornoway landed a crewman on the **Loke** to see if everyone was alright.

It was decided that the **Loke** would tow the **Strathisla** to Castlebay, Barra, where it was hoped the part time island fire brigade could extinguish the blaze.

Andrew Jnr. bravely went back aboard the burning boat to cut away the fishing gear so that the tow could commence.

As the **Loke** took the **Strathisla** on a stern tow
the lifeboatmen displayed great skill and courage by
keeping alongside her with fire hoses playing over
the engine room.

Myself, crewmates George Collett, Roger
Sargent and Andrew Jnr. were taken below to the
Loke's mess deck to be looked after by a caring
crew. Andy joined us later and had hardly sat down
when the German mate came in and said in heavily-
accented English:

"You have lost your boat."

Apparently, while making way through the
water, air had got into the engine room and fed the
fire with oxygen.

By the time we reached the **Loke's** upper
deck, the **Strathisla** was burning fiercely and it was
obvious to all that her death knell had been
sounded.

We were transferred to Barra lifeboat after
gratefully thanking the master and crew of the
Loke and she resumed her voyage to Stockholm.
The coxswain stood by the **Strathisla** for a further
30 minutes in case there would be a miraculous
chance to save her, but when we eventually left the
scene she was ablaze from stem to stern. I'll never
forget the sight of the **Strathisla** being consumed by
a multi-coloured funeral pyre as we steamed away
from her.

We were landed on Barra at 5.30 a.m. on
December 1 and a sorry looking sight we must have

looked. All we had left were the fishing clothes we were standing in, complete with seaboots. The local hotelier had been alerted and welcomed us into his establishment, where we had hot drinks and a bath. Later that day, Andy kitted all hands out with a complete new set of clothing and we caught the Oban bound **Lord of the Isles** ferry at 2 p.m.

Strathisla (CN 240) on the slip at Campbeltown shortly before the disastrous fire that finished her fishing career

Runs Ashore

ONE pleasant aspect of inshore fishing is the opportunity one has to widen horizons by visiting other mainland piers and the many islands, observing local customs and the different ways of life.

I have stepped ashore on 16 islands over the years and have become familiar with many people from Castletown on the Isle of Man to Castlebay on Barra. Getting ashore off the boat for a few hours works wonders, especially if the trip is a lengthy one.

The Isle of Man, especially in Peel or Douglas, is a wonderland in the summer months. It is easy to see why it is such a magnet for tourists, whose every whim is catered for.

I always look up fisherman Murdoch 'Sam' Morrison when in Peel. A Campbeltonian, he settled on the Isle of Man years ago and presently skippers the clam boat **Signora 2**. Whatever company we happen to be in, a word from Sam quickly ensures total acceptance among the

Manxmen.

Not far across the main is the Emerald Isle itself, where I spent three months fishing out of Portavogie, Co. Down, home of many friendly people amongst whom I was made most welcome. I ate often in the houses of my skipper, Fergie Hughes, shipmate Billy Sharp and my old friend Davy McClements. Fergie's wife, Adele, insisted on doing my laundry at no cost.

Another shipmate, Roy Bennett, coaxed a reluctant me to his Belfast home one weekend and I was, naturally, apprehensive at the thought of staying in the trouble-torn city. My fears were soon allayed for on the several visits I made to Castlereagh Road with Roy over the ensuing weeks I never once saw an act of terrorism or violence, which is confined mainly to certain parts of the city.

The club which Roy took me to on our Belfast sojurns had a curious custom of placing bowls of cold tripe on the bar counter and tables, in preference to the usual peanuts or crisps. The speed at which it disappeared was quite remarkable.

I used to think that the poor Irishman, so often the butt of music hall jokes, was being exploited unfairly. I am not so sure after witnessing a funny scene in Portavogie one day.

Billy, Roy and I were having a stroll round the village when we chanced upon one of the former's chums engaged in giving his car an oil change. The sump had been drained and the man was attempting to refill the engine with clean lubricating oil.

The only snag was that he was, genuinely, trying to pour the oil through the minute tube which held the dipstick.

"Boy this is wicked. I am going to be at this for hours," he commented.

We proceeded on our way and exploded into laughter on rounding the nearest corner.

I remember Billy showed me a postcard he had received from a friend who was on holiday. Written on the back were the words: "Weather here. Wish you were lovely".

Coming further north, we arrive at the Inner Hebrides and, as far as I am concerned, the diamond of them all – the Isle of Gigha. I have been visiting Gigha regularly for the past 20 years and I think I must know every one of the 180 souls on the three-mile long island.

My oldest friends on the island are Angus and Charlotte McAlister, parents of John and Archie the clam fishermen, who live in a trim cottage overlooking Gigha's main pier. Many a long winter's night was spent yarning with this contented elderly couple in front of a roaring fire, with perhaps an impromptu accordion recital by Angus included. I have watched fascinated as he made, without apparent effort, lobster creels in his big shed using traditional materials and methods.

Enforced stays at Gigha Pier due to bad weather always found me making for Angus and Charlotte's and my chilled bones were often warmed by platefuls of delicious home made soup taken from a veritable cauldron on the kitchen stove.

Dorothy Wilkinson, the wife of local fisherman Ian, is one of the island's district nurses and has many times attended to minor injuries sustained by visiting fishermen. Dorothy has a small VHF radio installed in her cottage used to communicate with Ian when he is at sea and times without number has taken calls from the boats with messages to be passed to Campbeltown by telephone. In return, skippers make sure she is well supplied with fish and prawns but Dorothy retaliates by sending mountains of home baking to the pier. Her chocolate sponges are particularly revered.

Seamus McSporran, who with wife Margaret runs the island's shop and a B & B establishment, is a remarkable character who has been the subject of several national newspaper articles. Seamus has teens of 'official' posts apart from his shop business, ranging from Special Constable to undertaker. How he finds the time to pursue all his activities is a mystery to me. Seamus is another extremely obliging chap who will drive the two miles to the pier with even the smallest grocery requisite.

One man I miss on my visits to Gigha is the

late James MacNeill, known better to Campbeltown fishermen as 'Jimmocks.'

Jimmocks returned to his native Gigha and lobster fishing in the late 70s after spending many years as an HGV driver on the mainland. He was self-appointed entertainments convener and I remember one evening he called at the pier to inquire if anyone was interested in attending a disco he had organised in the village hall. Half a dozen of us decided this would be a most welcome diversion and we piled into his beat up Morris van, with Jimmocks assuring us there would be a good attendance at the function. A total of 14 people turned up for the dance and even Jimmocks had to agree that 'two or three' more would have made it a better night.

Ever optimistic, Jimmocks had plans made for another disco the very next day. Sadly, Jimmocks passed on a few years ago.

Ken and Ila Roebuck, assisted by daughter Alison, ran the Gigha Hotel for a long time and were also good friends. Ken made it his policy to dispel the notion that wild drinking goes on 'willy nilly' on Scottish islands and was a master tactician when it came to persuading someone who had had 'one over the eight' to go home. The bar was closed promptly at 10 p.m. each night and did not open on Sundays.

The food in the hotel, prepared by Mrs Margaret Rose Graham, was second to none and I spent several long weekends between fishing trips in residence.

A visit to Gigha would not be complete without viewing the famous gardens of Achamore House, seat of the laird. Set down many years ago by the then owner, Colonel James Horlick (of the bedtime drink company), the gardens contain a comprehensive collection of tropical flowers and plants and are a blaze of colour during the month of May.

Across the sound lies Jura, which although much larger than Gigha, has roughly the same population. The island is dominated by three high hills known as 'the paps' and the local distillery's Jura Malt is a whisky much savoured by connoisseurs of the dram. A large number of red deer roam the hills and glens above Jura's main settlement of Craighouse, on the east side of the island at the head of the main pier. The walk from the pier to the village at night has to be exercised with extreme caution as it is one of darkest places I have ever encountered.

It was here on a suitably inky black night that, based on the highly questionable adage that it is every Highlander's right to take a deer from the hill and a fish from the burn, a master crime was plotted in the cabin of a Campbeltown prawner lying alongside.

A fish farm at the head of Craighouse pier had been in operation for some time and marketable fish were seen to be in abundance, jumping, twisting and turning invitingly in the farm's four tanks.

"Och, they'll never miss one buhlly", commented the ringleader as the motley crew made their way stealthily up the pier. An alarm trip wire situated strategically around the tanks was negotiated with ease and the landing net, left conveniently lying around, was soon bulging with four bonnie fish.

Excitement, however, got the better of one of the brigands in his haste to escape and he came into contact with the wire, setting off an audible alarm. An alsatian dog appeared out of nowhere and filled the air with spine-chilling barks, obviously intent on revenge. Fortunately for the three miscreants its attention was centred around the tanks and they made good their escape, albeit in extremely agitated frame of mind.

The fish were duly gutted, filleted and stowed in ice, ready for transportation to Campbeltown and their respective homes the following evening, which was landing night.

On approaching Kennacraig, West Loch Tarbert to land, our three heroes of hitherto unblemished character, were almost plunged into an apopleptic state by the sight of a Strathclyde Police car parked on the pier. Immediate action was required and resulted in the purloined fish being unceremoniously dumped into the boat's coal locker, to be got rid of later.

As it was, the policeman concerned was merely handing in a parcel for a colleague on Islay

at the Calmac Ferry terminal and he drove off
minutes later.

The sequel to the fishy caper that went wrong
took place the following night in the bar of the Jura
Hotel, when the fish farm manager, ever thankful
for a fry of haddock, informed the gang leader:
"Don't forget, any time you want a fish from the
tanks, just help yourself".

Another island I like calling at is Coll, though
I don't really know many of the inhabitants.

The first time I set foot on the island was
when fishing on the **Brighter Morn** with Tommy.
Another westerly gale forced us to give up fishing
on the Blackstone Bank, south-west of Colonsay,
and run for the shelter of Arinagour, the island's
main village. Though there was a living gale of
wind, the sky was clear with bright sunshine and I
took the opportunity of having a prowl ashore.

Not far from the ferry pier at which the boat
was moored I came across what could only be
described as a whelkers' paradise. In a gully on the
rocky shoreline was the thickest bed of periwinkles
I have ever seen. Unfortunately the tide was
flooding rapidly, covering the black shiny shells.

Shouting loudly, I managed to attract the
attention of colleague John Newlands on the boat
and told him to bring a sack as quickly as possible.
By the time John arrived, most of the winkles were
covered, but, between us, we gathered £30 worth in
20 minutes. Needless to say I didn't get the chance

to return at the next low tide.

John decided to explore farther along the shore while I had a contemplative smoke. Ten minutes later a breathless John was back, urging me to follow him and witness a commercially valuable find. He had stumbled on a massive trawl net, partly buried in the almost pure white sand, which must have been washed overboard from a big trawler during heavy weather. It was obvious that the net had seen little use.

Enlisting the help of a completely mystified holidaymaking couple from England, we eventually unearthed the complete net before making back to the boat for the remainder of the crew. It must have been a comical sight to see the **Brighter Morn's** crew, strung out at ten yard intervals, struggling across the machair with the netting draped over shoulders. Worth at least £2,000, the net was later cut up and used to make smaller trawls more suited to the **Brighter Morn.**

To end a completely profitable day, Tommy treated all hands to a bar supper in the island's hotel that night.

Of the mainland ports we visit, Ayr with its 'honest men and bonnie lassies' is a favourite. To me it is a very clean and well run town with an excellent shopping centre and I always look forward to landing there.

Tarbert, although a mere village compared to Ayr, must come top of the list. Again, over the years, I have made many acquaintances in the Loch Fyne port whom I can count on as being close friends.

They are a genuinely hospitable breed of men always willing to help me with fishing or other problems. They can also be dangerous if encountered in the various village taverns, pressing hospitality upon the unsuspecting visitor with gusto!

Men such as John McLeod **(North Star)**, John 'Tar' McDougall **(Nancy Glen 2)**, Ian McKay **(Prospector)**, James 'Jockus' Johnson **(Sunbeam)**, Kenny McNab **(Peaceful Waters)** spring to mind.

They are hard-working men who operate their own fishermen's co-operative with great success, including the sale of diesel oil, ice, chandelry, provisions and so on.

Of all the places it has been my privilege to see as a fisherman, the most naturally beautiful has to be Greencastle, Co, Donegal. Sited on the shores of Lough Foyle, this charming Irish fishing village is home to a considerable fleet of boats, ranging from cobles to 90-footers.

The words of that famous Irish song, *The Forty Shades of Green,* must surely have been penned in that locality when one looks at the fields among the rolling hills that dwarf the village, the colours of which range from the palest lemon to a deep rich bottle green.

Splints 'n Stitches

ACCORDING to information released recently, a fisherman is four times more likely to be killed at work than any other section of British industry. Indeed, more than 1,000 men have died at the fishing in the last 20 years. Tragic figures.

I myself have had my fair share of 'splints 'n stitches' despite making a conscious effort to be careful while at work.

One foul night in Kilbrannan Sound I was boxing herring in the fishroom of the **Alliance**. The boxes used at that time were the traditional wooden type and contained eight stones of fish, giving a combined total weight of nine and a half stones. A strong southerly breeze had whipped up a heavy bound, but as we were making northwards the boat was running before the motion in an orderly stern-on fashion. We had the boxes piled seven high when suddenly our neighbour boat, the **Crimson Arrow**, which was following astern, announced on the radio that they were going to shoot their net. As the **Alliance** turned beam-on to the sea to head

131

back south and pick up the end she began rolling heavily and a tier of boxes collapsed on top of me.

That little escapade cost me five cracked ribs and a fortnight ashore, heavily bound up.

On another occasion, while fishing for queen scallops with Ronnie on the **Bonnie Lass** off the Bennan Head, Arran, I received a nasty facial wound. Although the weather that day was anything but bad, there was an annoying spray when steaming free to windward while shooting the warps. I was at the winch, which was situated in front of the wheelhouse facing forward and bent my head to pull up the hood on my oilskin frock. The next thing I remember was coming to lying on the deck, and covered in blood. What had happened was that the heavy steel lifting hook block on the end of the gilson rope had worked its way free of its retaining bracket and had swung aft just as I lifted my head.

The resultant gash, luckily just below my eye, required eight stitches and a night in the Campbeltown Cottage Hospital.

Another 'sewing-up' visit to the same hospital came about after hauling the prawn gear with Nigel on the **Peaceful Waters** in the Ailsa Craig area. Procedure aboard this vessel was to take the trawl aboard with the power block at the completion of each tow. This operation was in progress when she took a roll and the net's centre, heavily weighted with chain, took a sender through the hydraulic

sheave and landed square on the top of my head.
Nigel, who was standing on my blind side, thought
that the dull thud was caused by the chain hitting
the deck and was amazed to see blood running
down my face. Mind you, I don't suppose there is
much difference between larch deck planking and
my sluggish brain. "Is the chain OK?" inquired a
concerned Bomber!

However, another five stitches administered
at the Cottage had me in one piece again.

One incident which, on reflection, I can now
laugh about after an interval of several years took
place just off Gigha's western shore while engaged
in clam fishing on the **Golden Fleece.**

The dredges came up absolutely crammed
with stones, in fact so full that they were actually
spilling out back into the sea. The towing bar had
to be winched down on to the deck (mentioned
earlier) and three of us stood on it to keep it there.
The lifting rope on the first dredge broke while
half-way up and it crashed back over the side. The
sudden jolt was enough to unbalance us and while
the other two lads managed to leap clear I was
catapulted into the drink as the bar sprang up. By
good luck conditions were perfect and I was
wearing only a light boiler suit. I was therefore able
to swim back to the boat, to be met with barely
disguised grins.

I suppose it must have looked kind of funny
at the time, me taking off in the direction of Jura

like a human cannonball. Never a dull moment.

I wonder how many times Archie McKellar Jnr., as he sits warm and comfortable taking bets in his father's Campbeltown bookmaker's shop, has contemplated the day he 'went over the side'.

Before becoming a turf accountant, Archie spent the first few years after school at the fishing, an industry his family had been involved in for a long time. He was at the Gigha prawn fishing with the late skipper Jamie Russell in the **Elsa.** It was in the pre-shelter deck days and Archie was sitting on the boat's rail, tailing prawns as the boat crossed in from the westward, rolling considerably in a heavy southerly motion. There is always one big wave that appears without warning and one such curler struck the **Elsa**, throwing Archie into the water. He told me later that it was the most frightening experience of his life, floundering fully-clad in boots and oilskins in a heavy sea watching the boat steaming away from him. Immediate action by skipper Russell meant quick rescue but Archie, despite being a strong muscular young man, was totally exhausted. As he says himself:

"If it had happened in darkness I would have been a goner."

One of the most serious accidents I know of in recent times involved my good friend and former shipmate, Tommy Finn.

He was at the herring pair-trawling with his father Cecil on the **Aquila** and the net was shot one night in the area around the Cumbraes, at the mouth of the River Clyde. It was Tommy's job to make sure that the net was clear and pass the combination wire sweeps to the other boat. As this operation is carried out as quickly as possible in case the herring shoal moves, and every man has his own particular position, nobody is quite sure what happened. But it was with horror they realised when the boats parted that Tommy had somehow become entangled in the sweeps and was in the water. As the boats spread out and the strain came on the gear Tommy was seen to be hopelessly twisted up in the double wire ropes, just like a pencil in an elastic band.

The pressure on his body was obviously intense, as was later ratified by the injuries he sustained. The boats closed together quickly and he was found to be unconscious when pulled from the water. After being put ashore at Largs, the nearest port, he was taken by ambulance to Greenock, where it was discovered he had a badly broken arm, caved in ribs and multiple rope burns. In addition, Tommy's eyes were completely red for a week or two. Once again, it was probably his strong physique which saved him.

The sea lock of the Crinan Canal at the Crinan end was the scene of another mishap I was involved in. We had just returned from a Tobermory-based clam trip in the **Golden Fleece** and were looking forward to a weekend at home.

One of the crew, Duncan Lang, scrambled up on to the quayside to make the boat fast in readiness for the opening of the sluice gates which would allow us to rise to the level of the canal basin and a safe haven for the weekend. The stern rope was made fast and then Duncan picked up the head rope.

Perhaps it was a case of slight over-exuberance on his part, but as he made for the bollard he broke into a trot. The bow rope, unknown to him, was still made fast on a cleat aboard the boat. When Duncan's end came taut he brought up, spun round and plunged straight into the canal. The fact that he was a non-swimmer and was dressed in heavy working gear was almost inconsequential compared with something else which was about to happen – the lock keeper was preparing to open the sluice gate, an act which turns the lock into a tumbling, whirling, chaos of water. Thankfully, I tossed a lifebelt to him and we hauled him to safety with nothing more than a bleeding nose where the belt had hit him. I shudder to think what would have happened if we hadn't managed to get Duncan out before the gate opened.

John Brown, formerly of the **True Token** (CN 298), and now an ambulance driver, I am sure, is still grateful to me for a bawling out I gave him as a raw lad.

Newly out of school, John came with us on the **Golden Fleece** while pursuing the Clyde prawn fishing. He was standing on the stern as the sweeps were being heaved in waiting for the trawl to break surface. I almost fainted when I looked aft and saw that he had his hand round the sweep, allowing it to run through. A split second after my stentorian yell to him to get clear, his glove – luckily a size too big – caught on a protruding piece of wire on the sweep and was torn from his hand. John watched its progress white-faced and traced it through a series of blocks and fairleads, finally finishing up wrapped round the trawl winch drum.

I'm willing to bet he didn't do that again.

I suppose I am lucky to be here today to recount an incident aboard the **Brighter Morn** in which I was inches away from being decapitated.

We were fishing among the sunken wrecks of North Atlantic convoy casualties, some 40 miles west of Ireland. Fishing there can be good, providing the gear runs clear of seabed obstacles of which there are, understandably, many.

As we commenced hauling operations at the end of this particular tow, it was realised that there was a weight on the port side of the net. Luckily no damage was done, but a large piece of ship's plating was seen to be jammed between the top and bottom ropes of the net. In order to take weight off the gear it was decided to lift the rockhoppers out of the water with the hydraulic crane. We would then have a better chance to free the obstruction. With the crane extended to its full height of 25 feet, the hoppers hung suspended like a monstrous string of onions.

What happened next is still unclear but the hoppers broke free and crashed to the deck. I was caught below on the back. Eager hands pulled me clear but a couple of minutes passed before I could speak a word, having been winded badly. Crewmates who had seen the incident told me later that if I had been standing a foot nearer the boat's rail my head would have been jammed on it and more probably removed by the hoppers. As it was, extensive bruising meant a fortnight ashore.

True Token (CN 298) tied up at the Old Quay, Campbeltown

The Welly and the Slipper

IT has been my pleasure to sail with certain men whom one could only describe as being 'characters' and who therefore amuse shipmates no end. In addition to their general repartee, often flavoured with a sprinkling of colourful language, the antics of these gentlemen sometimes borders on the hilarious.

One individual in this category is the redoubtable John Brown, or Bomber, whose philosophy of life at the fishing can be summed up in a few of his own words:

"Och, ye need a laugh at this job".

In his early thirties, Bomber is the latest in a long line of fishing Browns and is a highly capable seaman and competent fisherman. However, one of his many non-fishing attributes is the ability to capture seagulls with astonishing dexterity. I have often seen him catch up to five birds at a time.

One of his favourite tricks is to send the gulls to sleep, achieved by gently tucking the bird's head under one wing, folding both wings in and turning it in a wide, slow circular movement a few times. He once had 11 gulls lined up on deck in peaceful slumber. To release them is a simple matter of lifting the wings clear, whereupon take-off is undertaken with understandable rapidity.

Many seagulls have been ringed in recent years and another of Bomber's party pieces is to switch the coloured identification tags from the leg of, for instance, a large black back to a young herring gull, hoping for recapture by some dedicated bird-watcher.

"See the fella that ringed that gull, I'd laik tae see his face if he gets it back", he will announce on re-launch.

It must be made clear, of course, that no harm comes to the birds. Bomber is also a master of disguise and mimicry and while his carry-on never interferes with his work, he has relieved many a boring hour at sea with an impromptu showbiz performance. Mike Yarwood beware!

It is not uncommon for him to arrive aboard with some way-out mask concealed in his kit to scare the living daylights out of crewmates. I myself was confronted with a grotesquely deformed Alaskan bear wearing oilskins one pitch black night at the back of the **Alliance's** wheelhouse. His King Neptune act, utilising fine seaweed for hair and beard and a deck brush for trident, has also caused much mirth.

When he sailed on the **Alliance**, Bomber

regularly visited the wheelhouse with one object in mind – to pester my long suffering brother Robert and the result was often a jocular wrestling match. I have even seen them locked in combat whilst towing through a huge spot of herring.

On one occasion we were steaming home to Campbeltown after a successful week's fishing and everyone was in high spirits. Bomber started performing just as the boat entered Campbeltown Loch but Robert got the better of him by ordering him on deck to prepare mooring ropes. As he passed the wheelhouse the skipper sprayed Bomber with a liberal dose of a well-known aerosol rust repellant. Ignoring our guffaws, Bomber muttered something about war being declared.

Just as the **Alliance** drew alongside and with Robert's concentration directed fully on the berthing manoeuvre, Bomber darted into the wheelhouse and pulled the skipper's denims down to his ankles, exposing a set of underwear and a pair of short, fat hairy legs. Powerless to act, Robert had to complete the mooring-up operation thus, to his utter consternation.

My favourite memory of Bomber is of seeing him sprawling chest deep in a fish pound brimming with saithe, asking meekly for assistance to get out. It happened aboard the **Peaceful Waters** when, after a particularly big haul was made, he climbed on to the wheelhouse roof and although he had no such intentions announced to the assembled company that he was 'gaun tae jump' into the fish. At that precise moment, he stepped on a patch of slimy guana, the boat took a gentle roll and Bomber plummeted deckwards into the writhing mass. The peculiar fragrance which lingered about his person for some time afterwards was not entirely appreciated by his shipmates. A colourful character indeed.

Another of my favourite shipmates was skipper Colin Oman, with whom I fished for clams on the 40-foot **Boy David** (TT 78). While the Inland Revenue need not have worried unduly that I might scurry off to Switzerland and a numbered bank account, the 'crack' aboard with Colin was second to none.

The possessor of an agile brain, the popular Colin spent many years after university as a quantity surveyor before following his forebears to sea at a relatively late stage in life. He had a curious devil-may-care attitude, perhaps even touching on the eccentric at times. Colin bothered little about his appearance while at work and was the first to admit that the stout little boat needed "tidying up a wee bit". He once said to me:

"I have a haircut twice a year whether I need it or not", testimony to his thick mop of unruly curls.

Improvisation seemed to be the order of the day aboard the **Boy David** and when breakdowns of machinery occurred, they were ingeniously repaired using alien parts, whereas many a lesser man would have steamed to port for the services of an engineer.

During my first week with Colin, I noticed that the lifting tackle for the clam dredges consisted of an old U-shaped shackle attached to the end of the double purchase rope. This I eyed with suspicion, knowing that an appropriately heavy hook should have been in use. About the third day out the gear was almost aboard when, with an almighty crash, the towing bar chains and dredges half filled with stones came down about my ears and narrowly missed me. When I had recovered sufficiently from a state of near hysteria, Colin's calm comment was:

"That's funny, it worked fine for the last few weeks".

Our weakness was completing crossword puzzles whilst towing and a love-hate relationship developed between us when this was in progress. We argued with such vehemence over a clue one day while working in the Sound of Gigha that he actually put the boat in neutral and suspended fishing until the matter was resolved. Such altercations never lasted long, I am glad to say.

Gigha Pier was cluttered with boats as the **Boy David** drew alongside one evening and the wrath of a neighbouring skipper was aroused when it became clear to him that the noise of the overhanging dredges rubbing against his boat was going to spoil his night's sleep. To this end he demanded that fenders be put out to prevent such a happening, a non-existent commodity on the **Boy David.** Colin solved the problem admirably by producing a doubled over thigh wader and a plastic football encased in a piece of netting.

We did not normally work into the hours of darkness but nightfall descended quickly upon us at the close of a dark January day while fishing at Ardnamurchan. As we prepared to haul, I asked Colin to switch on the deck lights, at which juncture a torch appeared out of the wheelhouse window. It transpired that the only form of illumination on the boat were the port and starboard navigation lights. During the resulting pantomime a large seine netter making for Oban to land circled us and asked if everything was alright.

"Aye, aye", said Colin "the moon will be up soon". We berthed, however, at Tobermory half an hour later.

On one occasion Colin mislaid his shoes, though I suspect mischief on the part of a practical joker. Undeterred, he stepped ashore for his evening dram in a set of footwear which was, to say the least, unusual and he casually strolled into a hotel lounge wearing a carpet slipper on one foot and a wellington boot on the other.

No, I'll never forget life on the **Boy David,** spent in a permeation of cigar smoke, about 40 of which Colin smoked daily.

Another character to appear on the local
fishing scene was a young man with strong hippie-
type leanings. He graced his wrists with an

assortment of bangles and was quickly dubbed "piston rings".

One night his boat was landing in Ayr and he was detailed to barrow the day's catch of prawns from the boat into the covered fish market. En route he was asked by a fishing friend:

"Did you have many prawns today?"

Piston rings, looking acutely skyward, replied in dulcet tones: "Heaps man, heaps", and proceeded to propel both himself and the cart into Ayr Harbour. Fortunately he was fished out safely, but the several hundred pounds worth of prawns sank to the bottom, almost causing his skipper to suffer a coronary. Whether he had been using a certain additive to his cigarette tobacco is open to conjecture, but he certainly took a wrong turning that night.

Another local wag with whom I crewed only briefly but nevertheless worthy of mention is Andrew Wylie, or more commonly, Smokey.

He sailed with my father on the ring-netter, **Westering Home** (CN 259) and one summer evening as usual I was at the harbour to watch the fleet set sail. A fair amount of townspeople taking the evening air were also present and the sight of the **Westering Home** steaming out must have been viewed by them with incredulity. Smokey was on the starboard side of the boat and his chum, Andrew McSporran, on the port. Both were armed with 12-feet long fending off poles and appeared to

be rowing the 53-foot boat out of the harbour. My
father, always game to take part in Smokey's ploys,
agreed to set the boat on course and then kneel
down out of sight below the level of the wheelhouse
windows until they cleared the pier. Apparently the
main topic of conversation in the local bowling club
that night centred round the titanic strength of the
two young fisherman rowers.

Smokey took part in the Lamlash Loch queen
scallop fishery (mentioned elsewhere) and it was his
skipper's misfortune to net one of the dumped cars.
Following a struggle lasting for hours, the crew
were still having difficulty in getting the obstruction
strapped alongside and tempers were becoming
frayed. In an attempt to introduce a little light relief
into the proceedings, Smokey, with typical Wylie
wit, commented:

"They might at least have left the handbrake
off."

As it was, there was no suitable weapon within
handy reach of the skipper but had there been I'm
sure Smokey would have been nursing a tender
cranium.

Angus Durnan, better known as 'Wee Gus', is
another quick-witted character who has been the
source of much hilarity over the years.

Gus was skippering a 40-foot prawn trawler,
operating with one crewman, from Mallaig a few
years ago. One day he was listening in on the radio
channel reserved for communication to the

fishsalesmen's office while a huge trawler ordered provisions. He was staggered by the magnitude of the list – enough for an eight man crew for at least as many days.

It was obvious to Gus that the shore-based voice belonged to a very green young man, possibly a recent school leaver who had taken up employment in the office.

When the conversation was over, Gus immediately called the office, explained falsely that he had just arrived in the area and asked if he could order stores. The keen youngster told him to go ahead and Gus relayed the following:

"Two bantam's eggs; four slices of bacon; half a pint of milk; five Woodbine".

Gus and his crewman, Angus McGougan, had a good laugh to themselves thinking about the innocence of the earnest young trainee over the ficticious list but said:

"Nobody is that gullible."

Later that evening, Gus was ashore attending to the settling-up sheet for the day when he spied a tiny cardboard box bearing his boat's name amongst the rest of the fleet's stores. Sure enough, the items he had asked for were there, with a note included:

"Sorry, could not get five Woodbine. Hope 10 will do."

Alec Burnfield is another old friend of mine going back to our days as youngsters in the town's

Ralston Road.

Alec joined the fishing fleet straight from school as boy aboard the **Southern Sun** (B 53). He now successfully skippers the **Nostaw** (SN 48). It soon became apparent that a youthful Alec was, to put it mildly, a bit of a practical joker, and his escapades were many and varied, though not in any way malicious. I have long suspected him of being the voice behind a certain phantom character who makes infrequent radio broadcasts but I have no proof.

The **Girl May** was the scene of one of Alec's pranks involving a crewmate, Charlie McNaughton. Charlie liked to take his bicycle on trips which entailed calling at islands with remote piers to save him long walks to the telephone or shop.

Neil Kelly, the well-known marine engineer, had just completed a welding job on the **Girl May** and the boat set sail. After tidying away the mooring ropes Charlie remarked to Alec that he had better stow the bike, which was propped up against a stanchion, in a safe place before they reached the turbulent waters of the Mull of Kintyre.

"Och I don't think it'll go anywhere," said the bold Burnfield, with a twinkle in his eye.

Sure enough, when Charlie tried to remove the velocipede, it was found to be well and truly welded to the upright – a supreme piece of Burnfield artistry!

The Holy Boat

DERRICK Goode, a very old friend of mine, is a perfectionist in everything he does, be it work or play.

His adroitness at mastering anything he takes on is admirable, perhaps even, for me, maddening.

*Derrick Good's superb craftmanship can be seen in this beautiful model of Dunure, Ayrshire ring-netter **Marie** (BA 211).*

It came, therefore, as no surprise that when he announced that he was building a model fishing boat, the finished article was a masterpiece down to the last completely hand-made detail.

Though he had never before attempted such a venture, Derrick reckoned it would be the ideal solution to the problem of passing the time while ashore between berths.

During the vessel's construction, no amount of inducement would coax him into giving sneak previews of the progress but it was certainly worth the wait and I am proud to display the result of his painstaking labour in these pages, a perfect model of the **Marie** (BA 211).

Obviously to a man like Derrick, no ordinary timber would do for his model. It had to be something special and that is the way it was.

His friend, Joseph Brown, was involved with a firm which had the contract to demolish Campbeltown's Lochend Church at that time and Derrick asked him look out for a piece of wood which might suit the purpose. They met in Main Street several days later and Joseph reported that he had the necessary material at home. Derrick being Derrick, a taxi was hailed immediately which was just as well for Joseph appeared from his house staggering under the weight of a ten-foot section of pew back. Both the taxi's rear windows had to be wound down to allow the strange 'fare' to be transported to

Derrick's place, to the extreme dismay of the driver.

Two weeks and much sawing, chiselling and planing later, Derrick found his ideal two-foot length and he set about his task. He has since resisted many tempting monetary offers for the model and has no intention of selling, and has, in fact completed a further two beautiful examples of Clyde fishing vessels.

Stepping up a league, he has now completed the building of a 16-foot dory to help him fully indulge in his other passion of rod fishing.

Men and Boats

THE Campbeltown fishing fleet at the time this account was written (early 1992) was made up of the following boats and skippers.

Adoration (CN 78) skipper John McDonald
Amazing Grace (CN 289) skipper John Reid
Atlas (CN 258) skipper Andy Harrison
Bellemar (TT 76) skipper Richard Johnson
Brighter Morn (CN151) skipper Tommy Finn
Crimson Arrow (CN 43) skipper Jimmy McDonald
Glen Mave (SY 228) skipper Billy Wareham
Harvester (CN 200) skipper Archie Graham
Freedom (CN 194) skipper Campbell Keyte
Margaret Anne (INS 141) skipper Lawrence
    Robertson
Quiet Waters (CN 45) skipper Morris Shaw
Nostaw (SN 48) skipper Alec Burnfield
Nova Spero (CN 187) skipper Robert Gillies
Reynard (FD 48) skipper John McKerral
Stella Maris (CN 158) skipper Jamie Meenan
True Token (CN 298) skipper Joseph Brown

Chairman of the Clyde Fishermens' Association Campbeltown branch is Jimmy McDonald and secretary is local solicitor Mr Charles Reppke.

Campbeltown's focal point is its harbour and many local inhabitants take a turn round the quays at least once a week. Much improvement work has been carried out within the last few years, including extensive piling and the construction of a new fish market and office buildings.

Housed in the office block are CMC Fishselling Ltd, Carradale Fishermen Ltd, RNLI, Harbourmaster, HM Coastguard and the

Director Michael Durnan at work in the offices of CMC Fishselling, Campbeltown

Department of Agriculture and Fisheries for
Scotland.

CMC's offices on the top floor are a hive of
activity at weekends when skippers attend to the
business of 'settling up' with office manager Michael
Durnan. When this has been accomplished,
crewmen arrive in a steady stream to collect their
hard-earned wages.

Michael has little time to relax and puts in
hours more in keeping with his seagoing clients
which other office workers would view with
amazement. Arriving at the office at 10 a.m., he
does paperwork until 1 p.m. After a lunch break he
is back at his desk until 5 p.m., taking the many
radio messages transmitted by the boats on VHF
channel 45. A snatched meal sets him up for his
evening shift, when he prepares the boats' sales
tallies as they land. The frequent visits made by
Irish boats means that he can have as many as 30
vessels to attend to each night and it is often
midnight when he finally shuts up shop.

The two quays are kept spick and span by the
one and only Charlie Durnan, harbour attendant
extraordinary. Charlie, affectionately known as
'Dreesh' is a familiar figure to fishermen from all
parts and hundreds of yachtsmen. Conspicuous in
bright orange overalls and 'cheesecutter' hat,
Charlie's busy daily schedule includes a multitude
of chores, covering anything from catching
mooring ropes to touch up painting. The harbour

is a credit to him and woe betide anyone who leaves discarded fishing gear lying around in an untidy fashion on his coveted territory

The harbour master is former fishing boat skipper and marine oil supplier, Mr William McDonald, who was appointed to the post in 1990. He operates from a bright and spacious office with a fine view over the harbour and its approaches. Modern VHF radio enables him to 'talk' visiting vessels into designated berths.

The Scottish Department of Fisheries and Agriculture representative, or 'fishery officer' is Mr Jim Legge. Regarded by the fishermen as a kind of policeman, one of Jim's duties is to keep an eagle eye on fishing nets to ensure that the mesh size is not too small. The current minimum size for prawn trawls is 70 millimetres. Another of his roles is to inspect the various species of fish landed, checking for any that may be undersize. Infringement of fishing regulations carry stiff penalties and it is pleasing to note that defaulters in the Campbeltown fleet are few and far between.

A good and true friend to all Campbeltown fishermen is Peter McConnachie. Peter operates a shellfish processing factory in the town's Snipefield Industrial Estate as well as an ice plant within the modern fish market on the Old Quay. He unselfishly turns out at anti-social hours to meet skippers' ice requirements and gives, free of charge, widespread use of fork lift trucks and pick-ups to

fishermen for shifting heavy gear around. Yes, the
world could do with many more people of Peter's
calibre.

One service industry sorely missed these days
in Campbeltown is net-making, which disappeared
in the mid eighties with the retirement of Messrs
Charlie Flaws and John Shaw.

The Bridport-Gundry operations ceased some
years before that and the premises now house a
garage and car showroom. Charlie and John's
building has been converted into a block of luxury
flats. Consequently, nets have to be ordered from
elsewhere and come from places as far apart as
Fraserburgh and Fleetwood, which can cause
problems if the gear does not fish properly.
Discussion with the maker has to be conducted by
telephone, whereas in years gone by it was a simple
matter of the net man taking the offending article
back to the loft for alteration.

I have suggested to Andy Harrison on several
occasions that he set up as a netmaker in
Campbeltown. Andy makes most of his own prawn
gear and for years has been 'top dog' at the job.
Andrew Jnr. is now a fully-certificated and able
skipper and takes the **Atlas** to sea often with
excellent results. Perhaps we will see a much
needed net factory in operation in Campbeltown in
the near future.

VHF Howlers

The theory of electromagnetic waves – of which the radio wave is one – was originated by the British physicist James Clerk Maxwell in 1862. Not many people know that... The famous Marconi, of course, later developed the use of radio waves as a practical means of communication. I wonder if it ever occurred to the afore-mentioned boffins that the invention unleashed upon an unsuspecting world would spiral to such magnitude, especially in the maritime field.

Far from being a specialised piece of equipment aboard a boat nowadays the radio is an item taken for granted. VHF channels are never silent when the fleets are at sea. Apart from being used to discuss weather, fishing prospects and so on, conversations swing from matters marine to embrace a wide variety of subjects.

Some skippers, noted more for fishing skills than oratory prowess, have dropped the occasional clanger over the air and I would like to share a few of these little gems with you.

Names have been excluded for obvious reasons.

On describing: The spread at a buffet reception: "An' we had some o' them potato briquettes". The contents of the shipping forecast: "The man says the wind has tae rebate in the mornin." Activities during a naval exercise: "I see wan o' them nooclar sumbarines". Conditions in the wheelhouse on a hot day: "The respiration is runnin doon ma face." A near-accident on deck: "It's a good job his reflections were quick". The run of play during a televised rugby match: "The Barbicans were a' ower them." The proverbial Sunday lunch: "We had the provincial roast beef." The removal of an illegal trawl by the authorities: "Oor net was concentrated."

A dispute with the Department of Employment: "My case has tae go tae a tribuneral." A television pop music show: "Them physciatric lights were a' ower the place." The appointment of a Scottish university dignitary: "They voted him in as rectum." The introduction of a new piece of wheelhouse equipment: "Aye, it's a great invocation, right enough." The outcome of a court case: "He was remanded in custardry."

Sometimes VHF handset triggers jam on and, unbeknown to wheelhouse occupants, conversations meant to be of an extremely intimate nature are broadcast to all and sundry. Like the time two young watchkeepers were discussing at length, and in detail, the merits of a fisherman's daughter's anatomy. Her father, steaming along not five miles distant, heard every word. Sequel censored.

The best unintended transmission I ever heard was on the prawn grounds south-west of Gigha. The area is notorious for an abundance of minute nephrops, hated by deckies and loved by skippers. One chappie, hitherto not doing very well at all, took aboard 10 or 12 stone of the Ruskoline and was heard by all on channel eight to announce to himself: "My God, but you're clever McB."

Thank you James Clerk Maxwell.

Oban

THOUGH this book concerns my life as a Campbeltown fisherman, I have, courtesy of a lovely lady called Valerie, been 'exiled' for the past two years in the other main Argyll fishing town of Oban, where I was introduced to the world of 'wee boat' fishing.

Shortly after the **Strathisla** was lost I found myself with nothing to do and I therefore accepted with pleasure an offer from the well-known Mrs Zena Dickie to skipper her 37-foot prawn trawler **Sceptre** (OB 73). I did not quite realise the extent of the difference between big and small until one wild morning, while attempting to make a passage to Tobermory from Oban.

The wind was blowing from the south-west at about force six as the **Sceptre**, rolling violently, approached the infamous channel between Lismore and the Lady Rock en route to the Sound of Mull.

The **Sceptre** has a forward wheelhouse in which, to save space, the cooking facilities as well as navigational aids are installed. I was sitting in the helmsman's chair talking to crewman Danny Taylor who was standing behind me jammed against the door when with an almighty crash the calor gas cooker broke free of its mountings on the other side of the wheelhouse and was flung against my legs before disintegrating on the floor.

It was then that I realised that weather was an all important factor in small boat fishing and many days were lost in the early part of 1990.

This too is when I first encountered the plane graveyard between Kerrera and Lismore. The stretch of shallow water is ideal for small boats to 'pick away' on as the quality of the prawn caught there is second to none. The fact that there is a lack

*Wee boat fishing in the **Sceptre** (OB73)*

of bulk discourages larger boats from plundering it.

Though I had Decca readings kindly supplied by Alastair MacPhail of the **Friendly Isle** (LK 412) he warned me that the signal can go awry at night, and that it was better to use radar bearings to plot the sixteen planes that lie on the bottom.

Nearby Connel Airfield was used as a training base for pilots during the last war and whether the sunken aircraft were either ditched or scuttled in the sea I do not know. What I do know is that big prawns lurk close by them. It was while towing into the darkness one night that the boat's radar gave out just as the gear was slipping past one of the planes. Needless to say we came hard and fast. After a couple of hours it looked as if all was lost when one of the trawl warps parted, leaving us with one 10 ml wire connected to the gear. All or nothing, I decided, and gave the engine full revolutions ahead. To my surprise the net jumped clear and careful use of the winch eventually raised the resultant mess to the surface. We had actually torn one of the plane's wings clear of the fuselage and it was interesting to see that, after 50 years in the water, the red and black-painted aluminium was still in first class condition. The 'trophy' was stowed on the wheelhouse roof and was there for a couple of weeks before a scrap man bought it.

Lack of crew on the small boats can be a nuisance sometimes. Towing too close to the hard ground one day we lifted a huge boulder and took it into Oban. With me on the boat at the time was a chap known as 'Fleetwood Pete,' which was just as well because his surname was all but unpronounceable. The problem of disposal was neatly solved by recruiting Valerie to heave the stropped-up stone with the **Sceptre's** winch to the height of the boat's rail where Pete and I manoeuvred it into a dumping position. Immediately on pushing the stone over the side into Oban Bay, Pete and I instinctively jumped back to avoid the huge splash which followed. Not being familiar with such events, Valerie stood her ground and was rewarded with a head-to-foot soaking!

Several small boat operators actually fish the vessels single-handed. Although it is a practice I do not condone, I was forced to do likewise on the **Sceptre** when a crewman, incidentally very difficult to find in Oban, failed to turn up. Everything went well until the last tow of the day, between Kerrera and Mull, when the gear came fast.

By the time I managed to get everything aboard, the **Sceptre** was in four fathoms of water below Duart Castle. What would have happened if there had been an onshore breeze that day?

Like Campbeltown, Oban's fishermen are a close-knit bunch of lads always willing to help one another out and I have cause to be grateful to them for accepting a stranger into their midst and parting with Decca readings, pieces of gear etc.

The afore-mentioned Alastair MacPhail is known locally as 'Krypton'. The name stuck after Alastair was a successful contender in television's *Krypton Factor* programme, reaching the final stages.

Shortly after I arrived in Oban, Alastair was involved in a nasty accident which could have cost him his life. On awakening aboard the **Friendly Isle** early one morning he struck a match to light a cigarette. Unknown to him a leak had caused a build-up of calor gas through the night and the forecastle exploded in a ball of flame. Though he escaped with serious burns, Alastair reckons he is lucky to be alive. Part of his sleeping bag was later found caught up in the boat's foremast and must have been blown up through the hatch.

There are six bigger boats in the Oban fleet which follow the prawn fishing successfully in waters around Colonsay, Loch Linnhe and the Tiree Passage. As always, there is a 'top dog' in the fleet in the person of skipper Eric Groat in the 60-foot **Silver Dawn.** An Orcadian by birth, Eric made his home in Oban many years ago.

Also making a good job of things are Sandy Nicol (**Girl Zoe**); Johnny Scott (**Altair**); Angus McNeill (**Scarlet Thread**); Alan McGillivray (**Golden Years**); John Ogden (**Girl Norma**); Richard Anthwhistle (**St Mel**). The fishermen's howf in Oban is the Claredon Lounge, where manager Alan McKechnie and head barman George Ross hold court. Most of the crewmen on the huge fleet of boats which make Oban a base in summertime also use the Claredon and many tales are exchanged.

In common with all ports, 'characters' abound and in Oban's case the famous Mark McAllister is a kenspeckle figure indeed. Known far and wide as Marky Dan, he has often regaled me with yarns of some of the ploys he was implicated in.

He had me chuckling one day with his account of an incident on a 70-foot boat he was crewing on.

One particular haul produced an extremely valuable halibut which had missed the skipper's attention. Thinking ahead to landing time, Marky reckoned that the surreptitious sale of the halibut would provide excellent beer money for him and his colleagues until the 'settling up' of wages had been done. To this end, he packed the halibut in ice and hid it below the fish room floor. On arrival back at Oban the fish was forgotten about during the general bustle of landing and it wasn't until two weeks later, with the skipper on the point of calling in Rentokil, that the offending halibut was consigned back to the deep.